SEX IN ANCIENT ROME

Baltasar Rodriguez Oteros

Copyright

INDEX

Copyright 2
    FOREWORD 6
HETEROSEXUALITY. MARRIAGE 7
Forms of marriage 7
The divorce 9
    Cato the Censor (234 - 149 BC) 11
    Pompey 12
    Julius Caesar 12
    Mark Antony (83-30 BC) 13
Fulvia. 15
Clodia 15
Pompeii 16
OBLIGATION TO MARRY 17
Augustus and the Laws on Celibacy 17
Marriages of Convenience 26
THE WEDDING DAY 29
Virginity and Marriage 30
Text 31
HOMOSEXUALITY. GROUP SEX 34
Augustus and Caesar.Homosexuality 37
CATTLE. AGAINST CAESAR 40
Taunt Julius Caesar 40
ORAL SEX 44
Tavern Pimps 47
SEXUAL POSTURES IN ART 49
    Remedy Amoris. Sexual postures 52
Hair removal 57
UNDERWEAR 59
Indusium or Subucula (subuculae) 59
Camisia(Shirt) 59

Fascia and strophium(strophia) 59

The mamillare (mamillaria) 61

Subligar subligara subligaculum (from subligo, to tie underneath) 61

SEX TOYS. **62**

ADULTERY **66**

Julius Caesar's infidelities. Relationship with Cleopatra. 66

Accusations of adultery made by Marcus Antonius. 69

Catullus. Adultery. ad Gallum 71

Juvenal.Satires.Infidelities of the wife 72

PROSTITUTION **74**

MESALINE **82**

JUVENAL SATIRE 86

MARTIAL. SOME EPIGRAMMS: **101**

Chastity 101

Marriage of convenience 102

Prostitution 104

Taste for the forbidden 106

GREEK CULTURE REACHES THE MOST INTIMATE MOMENTS **106**

INCESTUOUS RELATIONSHIPS **110**

Incest.Ad Gellium LXXIV. 113

Incest.Ad Gellium 113

More on incest.Ad Gellium 114

Incest with his mother.Ad Gellium 115

BACCHANALIA **119**

VENERALIA **121**

SEX GODS **122**

Priapus 122

Mutuno Tutuno 123

Cinxia 123

Cloacin 123

Liburnum 124

Bona Dea 124

Faun/Pan 124

SEXUAL LEXICON **125**

POMPEII **128**

Lupanar or brothel 128

Suburban Hot Springs 130

BIBLIOGRAPHY **134**

Thanks 137

Author's review 146

FOREWORD

In this book we wanted to take a tour of the couple and
sexual life in the classical world: marriage, betrothal and
divorce, the wedding night, its parties, its gods, sexual
perversions, furious attacks against sexuality to denigrate
and manage to defeat the love or political rival, their false
morals and their misogyny, the wide and harsh world of
prostitution..., all these issues are rigorously treated
following faithfully the texts of the classic authors: Tacitus,
Suetonius, Catullus, Juvenal , the unforgettable Martial...
that tells us about the sexual life and personal vicissitudes
of historical figures such as Julius Caesar, Octavius
Augustus, Marcus Antonius, Messalina, Nero... and of so
many anonymous citizens, townspeople, in their lives loving

HETEROSEXUALITY. MARRIAGE

During the Monarchy and the Republic, marriage did not
have a formal character, it was a de facto relationship to
which the Law did not require a form for its constitution or
its extinction, not even the presence of witnesses,
magistrates or priests, and there was no publicity about it
because there was never a registry of marriages.
It became customary to prepare some **tabulae nuptiales**
(writing in which a relationship or inventory of the dowry is
made) that served as proof of the existence of a marriage,
although that was not its fundamental purpose.

To marry, it was required to be a Roman citizen, a minimum
age that
ensure sexual maturity
  -12 years for women.
  -14 years for the man and the consent of the
patresfamilias of both spouses (the authority of the **sui
iuris** over their families).

The only function of marriage was the procreation of
legitimate children,
ensuring the continuity of family gens and the worship of
ancestors **(sacra privata).**

Forms of marriage

There were two forms of marriage:
Matrimonium cum manu, by which the wife left her family

of origin and joined her husband's.

It was the most solemn to celebrate marriage among the patricians.

Confarreatio: Rite celebrated before the **Pontifex Maximus** and the **Flamen Dialis.**
A wheat wedding cake was offered to Jupiter. This marriage was indissoluble.

Co emptio: Simulation of buying the bride. The marriage of commoners.

Usus: declaration of will of both contracting parties and coexistence for one year (Roman de facto couples).
Matrimonium sine manu. The wife remained under the authority of her father. Usual since the end of the Republic since in case of divorce, the woman recovered her dowry.

The marriages were chosen by the paterfamilias. While the children continued to be alieni iuris, that is, being under the paternal potestas, the father could order their divorce if he wanted to, to remarry them according to his personal interests.

There was no freedom to choose a spouse for the **filii,** neither for men nor for women.

Neither men nor women were free to choose their spouse until, due to the influence of Christianity, together with the consent of the patres, the consent of the two spouses was required.

In ancient times, the **arra sponsalitia** was a guarantee that the promise of the future marriage (**sponsales**, nuptial) would be fulfilled; if the promise was broken, the deposit was lost.

In Roman Law they were considered as a special donation:

sponsalitia donation, an institution accepted by the civil codes.

It was the custom of the Roman nobility to celebrate the first marriage of their children at a very young age.
Parents promised their children when they were children in order to achieve economic benefit for their family with the sponsalia (promise of future marriage).
Although the man could join in marriage from the age of fourteen, it was not usual for him to do so until after he was seventeen, after having put on the virile toga.

It was very common for young people to barely know each other before the wedding. Sometimes, and surely for economic reasons, the bride lived in the house of the groom's family, before she was 12 years old, and was able to marry him.
In order for the woman to be able to marry, she had to give the groom an amount of goods and/or money, that the higher the groom's social position, the greater the dowry, since without a dowry she could not marry, unless the paterfamilias resigns. , something that was very rare.

The divorce

Until the end of the Republic the number of divorces was small.
Romulus passed a law that allowed the husband to repudiate his wife (note or libel of repudiation), but never the other way around, the woman could not repudiate her husband.
The first divorce that is recorded in the sources was that of the consular citizen Espurius Carvilius Ruga in 230 BC. who repudiated her wife because she could not give him

offspring and, therefore, was harshly censured (at that time, divorce was seen as worse than celibacy).

Until the second century BC., (end of the wars against Carthage) the marriage was contracted by means of the rite of the acquisition of the manus of the man on the woman: the wife entered the family of her husband.

Since that date, free marriage (sine manu) is generalized, a form that contemplated the Law of the XII Tables, the woman was not subject to marital power but to that of her own father.

This marriage modality, sine manu, and the influence of Epicureanism, which defended hedonism, caused the relaxation of the old customs and the number of divorces increased among the upper classes. Cicero laments that repudiation without cause is in common use.

The adulterium began to be a common practice among the Roman nobility, although it only carried a note of moral and legal condemnation when it was the woman who committed it. The consequence was the rejection of the woman by her husband.

Seneca states that some noble women counted their years not by the number of the consuls but by the number of their husbands.

We know from the comedies of Plautus and Terence that even plebeian family fathers promised their children in marriage and had the right to divorce them.

Among men, any public display of affection towards their partners was frowned upon.

The fact that a marriage lasted a lifetime was highly regarded by the Romans. The custom in nuptiae that a woman who had only had one husband (**uxor univira**) participate as pronuba or godmother, was a way of recognizing the values of marriage.

Celibacy was punished by the censors and men who had no offspring resorted to adoption, to marriages with younger women, with fertile women (who had already had children), or appealed to an old duty, based on amicitia and officium, by which a good friend could request the cession of the wife when she was fertile (before divorce and subsequent marriage), as Hortensius did with Cato the Younger and his wife Marcia.

The conservative ideas of the Emperor Octavian Augustus are reflected in the **Lex Iulia et Papia Popaea** that makes marriage a public duty, (as it was for the ancient Roman virtue), pursuing celibacy and childlessness (**orbitas**).
It forced unmarried men (**celibes**) between 25 and 60 years of age to marry, and women between 20 and 50. Otherwise, they were sanctioned with a succession disability that also applied to married couples without children (**orbi**).
The singles had a total inability to inherit by will and the orbi were deprived of half of their assets, the assets accrued to the heirs with children (**ius patrum**) and, failing them, were assigned to the public treasury, passed to the Condition.
Penalties were also imposed on widows and divorcees if they did not remarry.
The same rewards and punishments governed celibate and orbi to access public office.
It prohibited the nuptials of senators with actors or actresses and those of naive (born free) with women of low social status.
Citizens who complied with the Law could hold public office

before the required age, and were exempt from paying some taxes.

Augustus punished female adultery (not male) with banishment, he himself ordered his daughter Julia and her granddaughter to be banished to an island without men and without wine.

Cato the Censor (234 - 149 BC)

This politician and general, known for his tenacious opposition to Greek influence and staunch defense of traditional Roman morality, was a harsh husband, a stern father, and a master so cruel to his slaves that for him there was little difference between the treatment he gave to one or the other.

He married a noblewoman with whom he had an only son. On the death of his first wife, Cato being an elderly man, he lived in concubinage with one of his young slave girls, for this, his son withdrew his word.

With her he had another son, from whom her great-grandson will descend, Cato the Younger (a tenacious opponent against Caesar).

Pompey

When Sila takes power, he proposes to Pompey that he marry his daughter Emilia, who was already married and pregnant by her husband Glabrio (consul in 67 BC.), the marriage was short-lived, as Emilia died during childbirth. Pompey married for the third time with the daughter of the jurisconsult (and consul in 95 BC.) Quintus Mucius Scevola, who bore him three children, but Mucia's infidelities, taking advantage of her husband's absence, were in the public domain.

Cato adamantly refused to let him marry his niece, but Pompey had more success with Julia, Julius Caesar's only known daughter.

Julius Caesar

It was said that he had relations with the wives of his two colleagues in the triumvirate, Pompey and Crassus, with the queen of Mauretania, with the half-sister of Cato, his greatest enemy, or with the Egyptian queen Cleopatra VII.

Caesar preferred to go into exile, lose Cornelia's dowry and his position as **flamen dialis** rather than divorce his wife when the dictator Sulla demanded it.

The union would last fourteen years, until the death of Cornelia (69 BC.).

In the year 68 BC.Caesar married Pompeii, granddaughter of Sulla, a marriage from which he had no children.

In 62 BC. during the celebration of the Bona Dea festivities, Caesar being pontifex maximus, Clodius, disguised as a woman, was caught in Caesar's house intending to have an affair with Pompeii, a scandal that forced Caesar to disown her.

However, when Clodius is accused of violating the religious ceremony, Caesar refuses to testify against him, claiming not to know what happened. When asked why he had then repudiated his wife, he utters the famous phrase: his wife could not even be suspected .

Three years later (59 BC.) Caesar married Calpurnia for the third time, twenty years younger than him, from whom he also had no children. During this marriage, Caesar's absences were very prolonged due to his military campaigns, but her wife's love was proven by the fears that she showed in the face of the conspiracy that ended her life. A Tribune of the Plebs told of her desire to have offspring who commissioned her to draft a law that would allow him to have as many wives as he wished.

Caesar arrived in Alexandria chasing Pompey. As a result of his romance with Cleopatra, it is possible that a son, Caesarion, was born, with whom Cleopatra traveled to Rome at the end of the year 46 BC. where she resided until the assassination of Caesar.
Although paternity was taken for granted, the dictator never acknowledged it. Octavian, Caesar's sole heir, ordered Caesarion to be killed after defeating Antony.

Mark Antony (83-30 BC)

He was raised from the age of nine in the house of his stepfather Lentulus, (executed by Cicero as one of the ringleaders in the Catilina plot).
Appointed **magister equitum** during Caesar's second dictatorship, he was Rome's highest authority in the dictator's absence until the fall of 47 B.C.
When Caesar was assassinated, Antonius was Consul, which allowed him in November 43 to become a triumvir along with Lepidus and Gaius Julius Caesar Octavian (Octavian Augustus).
He was married three times and for years was the lover of Cleopatra VII. Cicero came to accuse him of having prostituted himself with men during his adolescence.

Antonio's second marriage was with Fulvia, a woman of great character who, according to Plutarch, dominated the general.

Cicero suggests in his Philippics that Antony and Fulvia were lovers in the life of the Tribune Clodius (her former husband).

Fulvia was already the mother of three children, Antonius had no legitimate offspring. To please Caesar's wishes and under the false pretext of adultery, he repudiates his first wife and marries Fulvia.

While Antonius is in Egypt, Fulvia confronts Octavian and must flee Italy to reunite with her husband, but she dies before achieving it.

Antonius offers Octavian the hand of Clodia, Fulvia's daughter with Clodio, but they do not marry.

Antonius did marry Octavio's sister (40 BC) Octavia, widow of the consul Marcelo with whom he had had three children. With Antonius he had two daughters.

He returns to Egypt in 37 B.C. and resumes his relationship with Cleopatra, eventually disowning Octavia in 32 BC.

Very upset, Octavian Augustus seizes Antonio's testament, deposited in the Vesta temple, and makes it public, so that the Romans make fun of Antonius, making him pass for a puppet in the hands of a foreign queen.

The union with Cleopatra was not a legitimate matrimonium (**iustum**) since it can only occur between Roman citizens, the only ones who have the ius **connubium** (right to contract legitimate marriage).

The marriage with Octavia subsisted by maintaining the **affectio maritalis,**
since she remained in the marital home taking care of Antonio's children (and also those he had had with Fulvia) and even traveled in search of her husband (35 BC), but Antonius sent her a delivery courier
for her to return to Rome.

Before disowning Octavia, Antony states that his

relationship with Cleopatra lasts nine years and that she is his wife: **uxor mea est**, reproaching Augustus that he also had lovers and that no one cared who they both slept with.

Fulvia.

A woman with a strong personality and political ambition, she was the wife of **Publius Clodius Pulcher,** who accused Cicero of the irregular process that sentenced some leaders of the Catilina uprising to death, which led to her exile. Clodio dies assassinated by political intrigues and Fulvia is widowed at 25 years old.
Shortly after, she remarries for the second time. Her husband dies in the civil war that pitted Caesar against Pompey.
She married **Marcus Antonius** for the third time, with whom she had two children.

Clodia

She was the sister of **Publio Clodio Pulcro**. Her first husband died under mysterious circumstances.
It is said that Clodia, the wife of **Quintus Cecilius** invited her friends to dinner when her husband was absent.

She had numerous lovers, including Celio, a friend of the poet Catullus, whom she accused of trying to poison her. Celio was defended by **Cicero**, who was very interested in the matter, since Clodia's brother was the orator's greatest political enemy, drunk and having had incestuous relations with his brother and Celio was acquitted of the crime although he had to pay bail.

Clodius accused Cicero's sister-in-law of incestum. He testified against Clodius at the Bona Dea trial. Clodius ordered the expulsion of Cicero in 58 and the destruction of his house on the Palatine.

Clodia also had Catullus as a lover, identified with the Lesbia of her poems, whom the latter loved deeply, but upset by her disdain, that she finds a new love, she bitterly regrets it.

Pompeii

Granddaughter of the dictator Julius Cornelius Sulla and second wife of **Julius Caesar.**

When Caesar is appointed maximum pontiff, residing in a domus publica assigned to the pontiff, his wife, has as a duty of office, organize the Bona Dea festivities, attended by the Vestal Virgins, in which the presence of men was prohibited.

A young patrician, **Publius Clodius Pulcher**, enters the house disguised as a woman with the intention of having relations with Pompeii. Accused of the crime of profaning a sacred place, Caesar does not testify against Clodius during the trial, and he is acquitted.

Caesar divorces Pompeii on the grounds that his wife must be free from suspicion.

Catulo.Crazy love
XCII.
Lesbia mi dicit semper male nec tacet umquam
Lesbia always talks bad about me and she never shuts up:

de me: Lesbia me dispeream nisi amat.
She let her die if Lesbia doesn't love me!

quo signo? quia sunt totidem mea: deprecor illam
By what sign do I know it? Because others such are mine: I curse her

assidue, verum dispeream nisi amo.
every day, but may she die if I don't love her!.

OBLIGATION TO MARRY

Augustus and the Laws on Celibacy

The **Lex Iulia de maritandis ordinibus**, proposed by Octavian Augustus, had a great opposition to be approved, it had to be modified, becoming the **Lex Iulia et Papia poppaea.**
He established a system of rewards and punishments, making marriage a public duty, as it was for ancient Roman virtue, pursuing celibacy and childlessness (**orbitas**).
In matters of succession, celibes and orbi were diminished or denied the ability to inherit;
the assets accrued to the heirs with children, (**ius patrum**) and in default of them, they were assigned to the public treasury.
The same rewards and punishments governed celibate and orbi to access public office.
It prohibited the nuptials of senators with actors or actresses and those of ingenuous women with low status.
The constant wars depleted the population of Rome. Only Roman citizens could be part of the legions. The State

requires that the birth rate be high so as not to have a deficit of soldiers. Octavian regulates these private institutions with these clear objectives:
the legions constantly need soldiers.
In Greece there is also this duty of the citizen to marry and have children for the protection of the State. Sexuality, the sexual act for exclusively reproductive and procreation purposes is a patriotic duty.
This state morality, embodied in binding laws, can never look favorably on sexual activities that only seek enjoyment, which is why oral or anal sex are rejected.
publicly, although, inside the domus, it is not exactly the same.

The traditionalist policy of Octavian Augustus, and his defense of the family and the birth rate, in accordance with primitive Roman morality, had its legal expression in a series of laws:
The **Lex Iulia de maritandis ordinibus** from 18 B.C.
The **Lex Iulia de Adulteriis Coercendis** of 17 B.C.
The **Lex Papia Poppaea** of 9 A.D.

-The **lex Iulia de maritandis ordinibus** (Julia law of class marriage) of 18 B.C. encourages marriage and childbearing, protecting the senatorial nobility by limiting marriages between social classes, punishing the celibate (single) and benefiting the married according to their number of children.
Rejected out of hand, it had to be modified and softened.
It established that the lying inheritance, in case of lack of heirs, would fall in favor of the State.

-The **lex Papia Poppaea** set the ages for marriage:
25 to 60 years for men; 20 to 50 years for women.

Those who had not married in those ages would be declared celibate, they would be sanctioned financially, and they would be deprived of their quota or portion in the inheritances.

Interestingly, the consuls who proposed it (**consules suffecti**), Papio Mutilo and Poppeo Secondo, were celibate.

The marriage of a senator (or the children of a senator) with a freedwoman (emancipated slave), or with a woman whose father or mother had exercised an **ars ludica** (dancer, flutist, actor or gladiator), with a prostitute was prohibited , or the marriage of a freedman with the daughter of a senator.

If someone donated or bequeathed something under the condition of not getting married, the condition was considered not set.

It was possible to donate or leave as an inheritance under the condition of not marrying certain person(s), whom the donor or testator judged inappropriate for the donee or heir; or under the condition of marrying a certain person, if the marriage was legally possible, otherwise the condition would be considered null and void.

To favor marriages, those who continued to live in celibacy after a certain age were sanctioned. **Celibates** could not receive an inheritance or legacy.

If a person was caelebs at death, the testator would only receive the inheritance or legacy if he married within the following 100 days, otherwise his hereditary rights would expire in favor of the State.

Widows had a period of one year (**vacatio**) after the death of their husband, and divorced women, six months after the divorce; to marry and be able to inherit, without sanction. Later, these terms were extended to 2 years for widows, and to 1 year and a half for divorcees.

-A **Senatus consultum Claudianum** softened the rigor of the new norms:
•A man who married a woman under 50 after the age of 60 was not punished.
•If the man was under 60 and the woman over 50, at the death of the woman, her dowry was considered expired.
According to the Law, a suitor who had several children was preferred to one who had few or none.
•Freed women who had four children freed themselves from the protection of their employers.

Women were exempt from the position of curator:
•that they had three children if they lived in Rome.
•that they had four if they lived in Italy.
•that they had five if they lived in the provinces.

The Senate or the emperor sometimes granted celibates the same privilege as those who had children (**ius liberorum**).
Pliny affirms that he obtained from the emperor, for a friend of his, the **ius trium liberorum** (right of the three children), likewise the poet Martial*.
* Titus and Domitian granted him the right of the father of three children and he was made an honorary military tribune, for which he acceded to the ordo equester (knight).
Antoninus Pius established that children must be registered and inscribed with his name in the **Praefectus Aerarii Saturni** within thirty days after their birth.
The law also imposed sanctions on orbis, (married couples

who had not had children between the ages of 25 and 60 for men and between 20 and 50 for women).

The **orbis** only received half of the inheritance or legacy. These provisions were attempted to be circumvented by many through fraudulent adoptions or even child abduction, so much so that a Senatus consultum of Nero declared them null.

The spouses could leave to a third party, as part of their free disposal, up to 1/10 of their assets; something that depended on the number of children born in the marriage or in another marriage, so that they could freely dispose of a larger share of the inheritance.

The conservative ideas of Emperor Octavian Augustus are embodied in this law, which due to its severity, was tried to avoid.

Suetonius, Lives of the Twelve Caesars XXXIV.
Augustus establishes the obligation of every citizen to marry for the subsistence of the Republic (of the Empire), something that already existed in the Greek city-states, everything was done for the good of the State. We can remember what was said about Socrates in this regard. Marriage (and subsequent procreation) was considered more of a legal obligation than a personal desire.
This is how Suetonius tells us in Life of the Twelve Caesars:

Leges retractavit et quasdam ex integro sanxit,
He revised all the laws and made some of them absolute,

ut sumptuariam et de adulteriis et de pudicitia, de ambitu, de maritandis ordinibus.
such as sumptuary and those that existed against adultery,

immorality, intrigue and celibacy.

Hanc cum aliquanto severius quam ceteras emendasset,
prae tumultu recusantium perferre non potuit,
As for this one (referring to the law of celibacy), which he
made even more severe than the others, the violence of the
protests it caused prevented him from keeping it,

nisi adempta demum lenita(ve) parte poenarum,
he being forced to suppress or sweeten part of the
penalties,

et vacatione trienni data auctisque praemiis.
to grant a term of three years and even to increase(increase)
the rewards.
lit.y given(granted)/(by)giving a dispensation of three years
and increasing the...

Sic quoque abolitionem eius publico spectacle pertinaciter
postulante equite,
Although the law was reformed in this way, the gentlemen
shouted for its abolition in the middle of the show;
also asking tenaciously for the order of the knights its
abolition in the show.

acctitos Germanici liberos receptos que partim ad se
partim in patris gremium ostentavit, manu vultuque
significans ne gravarentur imitari iuvenis exemplum.
[Augustus, then, calling the sons of Germanicus, who came,
some to his arms, and others to their father's, and showing
them to the people, exhorted them with attitude and look

not to be afraid to imitate the example of that young prince].

Cumque etiam immaturitate sponsarum
choosing brides who could not marry for a long time

et matrimoniorum crebra mutatione,
and frequently changing wives,

vim legis eludi sentiret,
Noting later that the provisions of the law were flouted,

tempus sponsas habendi coartavit, divortiis modum
imposuit.
he restricted the duration of betrothals and limited the
freedom of divorces.

Here we have three epigrams of the Hispanic poet Marcial
where he satirizes the false social puritanism that Octavian
Augustus intended to bring.

Book 6.7
Iulia lex populis ex quo, Faustine, renata est
Since the law Julia, Faustino, has been reborn for the
people

attack intrare domos iussa Pudicitia est,
and Modesty has been ordered to enter the houses,
and chastity has been commanded to enter houses,

aut minus aut certe non plus thrice lux est,
Thirty days have passed or less or surely not more,

et nubit decimo iam Telesilla uiro.
and Telesila is already married to her tenth husband.

Quae nubit totiens, non nubit: adultera lege est.
The one who marries so many times does not marry, she is
an adulteress in accordance with the law.

Offendor moecha simpliciore minus.
It bothers me less a prostitute more clearly.

In this other, he adds:

22
Quod nubis, Proculina, concubino
Because you marry your concubine

et, moechum modo, nunc facis maritum,
and make the adulterer until yesterday your husband today,

ne **lex Iulia** te notare possit:
so that the Julia law cannot condemn you,

non nubis, Proculina, sed fateris.
you don't get married, Proculina, but you plead guilty.

6.45

Lusistis, (satis est): lasciui nubite cunni:
You have enjoyed. (Enough already). Get married, lewd
pussies:

permissa est uobis non nisi casta Venus.

you are allowed nothing but chaste love.

Catullus.False chastity

LXX

Nulli was dictated mulier mea nubere malle
My wife says that she prefers not to marry anyone
My wife says that she prefers not to give herself to anyone

quam mihi, non si se luppiter ipse petat.
more than me, not even if Jupiter himself asks him to.

Dicit: sed mulier cupido quod dicit amanti,
He says so: but what a woman says to a passionate
(anxious) lover,

in vento et rapida scribere oportet aqua.
in the wind and in fast-flowing water, it is convenient to
write it down.
in the wind and in a stream of water should be written.

No one was as loved as you

LXXXXVII.
Nulla potest mulier tantum se dicere amatam
No woman can say that they have loved her

vere, quantum a me Lesbia amata mea est.
really as much as I have loved you, Lesbia.

nulla fides ullo fuit umquam foedere tanta,
There was never in any pact such a great loyalty,

quanta in amore tuo ex parte reperta mea est.
like the one I have put on my part in my love for you.

Marriages of Convenience

10

Petit Gemellus nuptias Maronillae,
Gemelo asks for marriage to Maronila,

et cupit et instat et precatur et donat.
and he wants her and hounds her and begs her and offers
her gifts.

Adeone pulchra est? Immo foedius nil est.
Is she so pretty? Yes, there is nothing uglier.

Quid ergo in illa petitur et placet? Tussit.
What does he seek, then, and does he like her? cough
Note. In this epigram, the poet Marcial criticizes the seekers
of inheritances or fortune seekers.
Young boys from noble families who came to less and who
intend to marry very old or seriously ill women who have
sufficient financial resources waiting to soon become their
heirs.

XXIII
Nubere Sila (feminine) mihi nulla non lege parata est;
Sila is willing to marry me not without conditions;

sed Silam nulla ducere lege volo.
but I don't want to marry Sila under any conditions.

Cum tamen instaret, "deciens mihi dotis in auro
However, as she insisted, (I said: You will give me) a million
gold as a dowry as a wife.

(sponsa dabis" dixi. "Quid minus esse potest?"
  What else could she be?

"Nec futuam quamvis prima te nocte maritus,
I will not make you as a husband even the first night,

communis tecum nec mihi lectus erit;
and I will have no fellowship with you.

complectarque meam, nec you prohibit, amicam,
And I will hug my lover and you will not forbid me,

ancillam mittes et mihi iussa tuam.
and, when I command you, you will send me your slave.

te spectante dabit nobis lasciva minister basia,
Before your very eyes, a young slave will give me lascivious
kisses,

sive meus sive erit ille tuus.
if he is mine as if he is yours.

Ad cenam venies, sed sic divisa recumbes,
You will come to dinners, but you will lie down at the table
so distant,

ut non tangantur pallia nostra tuis.
that my mantle does not touch with yours.

Oscula rare dabis nobis et non dabis ultro,
You will give me a kiss from time to time and you will not
give it to me on your own initiative,

nec quasi nupta dabis sed quasi mater anus.
neither will you give it to me as if you were my wife, but as if
you were my old mother.

Si potes ista pati, si nil perferre recusas,
If you can take this, if you can't resist taking it all,
Invenies qui te ducere, Sila, velit."
you will find, Sila, whom she wants to marry you.

3. 4
Cum placeat Phileros tota tibi dote redemptus,
You liking (the young) Fíleros, you bought him with all your
dowry,

tres pateris nato, Galla, perire fame.
consent, Gala, that your three children starve.

Praestatur cano tanta indulgentia cunno,
So much consideration has a cunt with gray hair,

quem nec casta potest iam decuisse Venus.

who is no longer fit for even a chaste love.
to whom not even a chaste love can go to bed.

Perpetuam di te faciant Philerotis amicam,
May the gods make you forever the bribe of Fíleros,

or mater, qua nec Pontia* deterioration.
oh mother even worse than Poncia!.
* Woman who, according to Juvenal, killed her children.

THE WEDDING DAY

The day of celebration was chosen very carefully; it was bad
to marry in the third week of February, the first fortnight of
March, in the entire month of May, the first fortnight of June,
the disastrous days, the Kalends, Nones, and Ides. The ideal
time was the second half of June and a Friday, a day
consecrated to Venus, the goddess of beauty and love.
On the eve of the celebration, the woman consecrated her
girl's toys to the gods of her house; afterwards, she went to
bed in her wedding dress. Her costume was a white tunic
with a double wool knot belt, **cirgulum herculeum**, she
covered her head and face with an orange veil, **flammeum**,
that covered her face; on her head, a crown of flowers or
metal.

The future wife was assisted by the godmother, pronuba, a
matron married only once, **uniuira**.
The tabulae nuptiales were signed by the contracting
parties and ten witnesses, (they were the record of proof of
the dowry and its restitution if the marriage was dissolved).

The **pronuba** put her right hand, **dextratum inuctio**, and the contracting parties said: ubi tu Marcus ego, ubi tu Silvia ego; Rings were placed on the ring finger in the belief that it was linked to the heart.

After the wedding banquet, the husband accompanied the wife to her parents' house (**uxorem ducere**) where an abduction was faked.

Then they went to the house of the husband who asked the wife what her name was, she answered with the nuptial formula: ubi tu Gaius, ibi ego Gaia, if you Gaio, I Gaia, (in a freer translation: wherever you are, there I will be me).

Her companions lifted her up so that her feet did not touch the doorjamb and they took her home. The children threw nuts at the bride and groom.

The guests returned to the houses. The next day an intimate banquet (**repotia**) was held for the relatives of the husbands, the wife received gifts from the husband and her family.

Virginity and Marriage

On the eve of the celebration, the woman consecrated her girl's toys to the gods of her house; afterwards, she went to bed in her wedding dress.

Her costume was a straight white tunic, woven by herself, with a double-knotted belt of wool (**cirgulum herculeum**). Her head and face were covered with an orange veil (**flammeum**) to attract luck and ward off evil spirits; on her head, a crown of flowers or metal.

When Christianity was consolidated, women who wore almost transparent silk dresses were attacked for lack of modesty:

"That they do without the ornaments, the braids in the fabrics, the gold thread and the silks... it is not a delicate

protective dress, since it is not capable of covering nudity."
(Clemente).

An element of the bride's dress is the belt (**cingulum**) held
by the Hercules knot, a belt that the **pronuba** (godmother)
girded the bride and that her husband untied in the lectus
genialis.

The belt symbolizes the virginity of the wife and the union
of the couple.
The Hercules knot (plain or curl knot) was made to protect
from all evil that threatens the purity of the bride and favor
her fertility. Difficult to untie, it is represented in belts, rings,
brooches, diadems...

According to Macrobius, it favored the fertility of the couple,
the symbolic union man-woman to reproduce, which is
formed by the two serpents of the caduceus of Mercury, as
represented in the myth of Tiresias.

Seneca in her letter to Lucuilio refers to the protective value
of the knot:
Bonum animum habe : unus tibi nodus sed Herculaneus
restat
Take heart: you only have one knot left, but it's Hercules'.

Pliny in his Natural History says that if wounds are covered
with a bandage tied with this knot, they heal much faster.
Vulnera herculaneum node praeligare, mirum quantum odor
medicine est
It is surprising to what extent tying wound bandages with
the Hercules knot leads to faster healing

Text

Cingillo noua nupta praecingebatur quod uir in lecto soluebat,
The bride was bound by a belt that her husband untied in her bed.

factum ex lana ouis, ut sicut illa in glomos sublata
was made of sheep's wool, and meant that, like wool divided into fleeces,

Coniunctainter se sit, sic uir suus secum cinctus uinctusque esset.
She was united with each other, so also the husband was bound and united.

Hunc Herculaneum node uinctum uir soluit ominis gratia,
this belt with the Hercules knot the husband untied,

ut sic ipse felix sit in suscipiendis liberis
as an omen that he will be happy with the birth of so many children

ut fuit Hercules qui septuaginta liberos reliquit.
as had Hercules, who was the father of seventy.

Eurystheus entrusts Hercules as work number eleven, the gold belt that Ares gave to his daughter Hippolyta, queen of the Amazons, warrior women, under the protection of Artemis, goddess of the hunt.
Received with kindness, the queen promises to give her the belt. This causes a tremendous anger of Hera (Juno) who, pretending to be an Amazon, shouts that what Hercules and

his men were really looking for was to kidnap the queen. Finally, the hero killed Hippolyta and he snatched his precious belt.

Honey could not be missing on the wedding night (to regain strength
for the ardor of love, that's where honeymoon comes from) and a few branches of mint or peppermint, which was considered an aphrodisiac herb.

The newlyweds consummated the marriage and to ensure that this happened, if the husband's nerves prevented it, the wife herself would use a wooden statuette of the god **Priapus**, the phallic god of fertility.
To help ensure that on their wedding night no woman was left without deflowering, fearing the lack of virility of some inexperienced man, the newlyweds used leather dildos in the shape of a male penis, which represented Priapus, the phallic god of vigor. sexual.
There were not many preliminaries or caresses, which if excessive could be interpreted as effeminacy or little manhood of the husband.
Sex was practiced in the dark and at night. It was very frowned upon to make love during the day (a privilege that only newlyweds had on their honeymoon).
Sexual pleasure should be exclusive to the one who penetrates, to the vir, which is why moans or displays of female pleasure were rejected and had to be repressed by married women (midwives).

HOMOSEXUALITY. GROUP SEX

-In the **Annals** of **Tacitus** the practice of passive male homosexuality by a Roman citizen is shown:

"They accused him of having committed many dishonesties with the soldiers whom he won over with money... adultery with Poppea and coming to do the job of a woman with her body (that is, he had been anally penetrated)" .

- In one of Luciano's Dialogues female homosexuality or lesbianism appears. A zither player is the lover of two rich women:

"They had hired me to play the zither for them... Megila tells me: come on, it's a good time to go to bed, so get into bed with us, between the two of us... They kissed me like men opening the door a crack. mouth, while they squeezed my breasts... I don't need men at all, because I have something in exchange for virility; you'll see".

The same prostitutes rejected lesbianism:

-" I heard that Megila, the rich lesbian, is in love with you, that you live together and that I don't know what things you do to each other.

- "It's true, and I'm ashamed myself."

In Homer's Iliad, the word Lesbos appears to refer to women who performed oral sex on men. The prostitutes on the island of **Lesbos** were known for such sexual activity. Since the poet Sappho was homosexual and lived on Lesbos, the term changed in meaning. In Greece, female homosexuality is called tribada, from tribo (to rub).

"The old man arrived accompanied by a girl who told me, don't be afraid, come with me... you can choose between being active or passive... the group was so excited that I thought they had taken the aphrodisiac called satyrion; when they saw us they adopted much more lascivious...".

Roman public morality, much more conservative than the Greek, rejected sexual relations between men. Performing anal sex with another man (being accused of having been anally penetrated by another man), was public **infamy**.

Suburban Baths, Pompeii.Apodyterium.Scene VI.

Martial, Epigrams.

71

Mentula cum doleat puero, tibi, Naeuole, culus,

If your slave's turnip hurts and you, Névolo, your ass,

non sum diuinus, sed scio quid facias.

I'm no fortune teller, but I know what you're doing.

Catullus

LVI.

ad Catonem

O rem ridiculam, Cato, et iocosam,

Oh, laughable thing, Cato, and funny

Dignamque auribus et tuo cachinno!

and worthy of your ears and your laughter!

ride quidquid amas, Cato, Catullum:

Laugh, Cato, as much as you love Catullus:

res est ridicula et nimis iocosa.

the thing is laughable and very funny.

sorprendi modo pupulum puellae [trusantem]*

I surprised a young man who was pushing (he was banging) a girl:

[*]; hunc ego, si placet Dionae,

to him I, with forgiveness of Dione,

protellus rigida mea cecidi.

I hit him with a stiff mine.

LXIII
Ad cenam invitant omnes te, Phoebe, cinaedi.
They invite you to dinner, Febo, all the queers.

mentula quem pascit, non, puto, purus homo est.
Whoever feeds his prick is not, I believe, a pure man
(without blemish).

Something that was used as a means to eliminate political
rivals. This is what Marcus Antonius tried with Octavian
Augustus or the Poet Catullus who accused Julius Caesar.
Although hypocritically, many of these same accusers
maintained, behind closed doors, relations with their slaves,
with their friends, or even paid young minors to carry
outsexual activities.
For example, Catullus himself.

Augustus and Caesar.Homosexuality

Suetonius recounts in his Lives of the Twelve Caesars:

LXVIII.

Prima iuventa variorum dedecorum in famiam subiit.
Various opprobriums stained his reputation (that of
Octavian Augustus) from a young age.

Pompeius ut effeminatum insectatus est;
Pompey called him effeminate.

M. Antonius adoptionem avunculi stupro meritum;
M. Antonius censured him for having bought his uncle's adoption at the price of his dishonor;

item Marci frater, quasi pudicitiam delibatam a Caesar,
Marcus Antoniu's brother claimed that after giving Caesar the flower of his youth,

etiam in Hispania trecentis milibus nummum substraverit,
he sold it again in Spain for three hundred thousand sesterces,

XLIX.
Caesar's homosexuality was harshly criticized by all his enemies.
Although, certainly, he was bisexual, something frequent in the Greco-Roman world, especially among the upper classes.

Pudicitiae eius famem nihil quidem praeter Nicomedis contubernium laesit,
His intimate acquaintance with Nicomedes constitutes a stain on his reputation,

gravi tamen et perenni obprobrio et ad omnium convicia exposito.
that covers him with eternal disgrace and for which he had to suffer the attacks of many.

Omitto Calvi Licini notissimos versus:
I omit the well-known verses of Calvo Lucinio:

Bithynia quicquid et pedicator Caesaris umquam habit.
Everything Bithynia and Caesar's lover ever owned.

Bithynicum fornicem'
Bithynian prostitute.

Cicero vero non contentus in quibusdam epistulis
scripsisse a satellitibus eum in cubiculum regium eductum,
Not satisfied with Cicero having written in some of his
letters that Caesar was carried into the royal chamber by
soldiers,

in aureo lecto veste purpurea decubuisse,
that he lay in her covered in purple on a bed of gold,

floremque aetatis a Venere orti in Bithynia contaminatum,
and that in Bithynia that descendant of Venus prostituted
the flower of his age,

quondam etiam in senatu defendenti ei Nysae causam,
filiae Nicomedis, benefique regis in se commemoranti:
he told him one day in full Senate, and when [Caesar]
remembered the favors he owed to this king:

'remove,' inquit, 'istaec, (I pray you), [quando notum est,
Omit, he said, (I beg you), all that, because, since (it is
known),

(et) quid ille tibi (et) quid illi tute dederis].
what you received from him and what you have given him.

' Gallico denique triumpho milites eius

And finally, on the day of his triumph over Gaul, the soldiers,

inter cetera carmina, qualia currum prosequentes ioculariter canunt,
among the verses with which they usually celebrate the march of the winner,
Literally, among the other verses with which they sing gracefully accompanying the triumphal chariot,

etiam illud vulgatissimum pronuntiaverunt:
the well-known sang:

Nicomedes Caesarem. Gallias Caesar subegit,
Caesar subdued Gaul; Nicomedes to Caesar.

Ecce Caesar nunc triumphat
Here is Caesar who triumphs [because he subdued Gaul],

Nicomedes non triumphat, que subegit Caesarem.
while Nicomedes who subdued Caesar does not triumph.

CATTLE. AGAINST CAESAR

Taunt Julius Caesar

XXIX.
in Romulum cathamitum.
Homosexual man or with feminine features.
*cathamitum cathamiti, qualifier of Ganymede, young cupbearer and lover of Jupiter.

Quis hoc potest videre, quis potest pati,

Who can see this, who can stand it,

nisi impudicus et vorax et aleo,
Unless he's a brat, a devourer and a player,

Mamurram habere quod Comata Gallia
May Mamurra possess what hairy Galia used to

habebat uncti et ultima Britannia?
possessed and the confines of Britannia?

cinaede Romule haec videbis et feres?
Rómulo queer, will you see and endure this?

et ille nunc superbus et superfluens,
And he now, haughty and overflowing,

perambulabit omnium cubilia,
he will go through everyone's rooms,

ut albulus columbus aut Adoneus?
like a white dove or an Adonis?

cinaede Romule, haec videbis et feres?
Romulo queer, will you see and endure this?

he is impudicus et vorax et aleo.
You are shameless, a devourer and player.

eone nomine, imperator unice,
And with those credentials, peerless general,

fuisti in ultima occidentis insula,
you were in the farthest island of the West,
* Refers to his campaign in Britannia (present-day Great Britain).

ut ista vestra diffututa mentula
so that your flaccid dick

ducenties comesset aut trecenties?
he devoured two or three hundred thousand sesterces?

quid est alid sinistra liberalitas?
What else is that disastrous generosity?

parum expatravit an parum elluatus est?
Did he squander little or did he squander little?

paterna prima lancinata sunt bona,
The first, ended with his paternal assets;

secunda praeda Pontica, inde tertia,
then, with his spoils from Pontus; thirdly,
*War against the Parthians.

Hibera, quam scit amnis aurifer Tagus:
with the Iberian, which knows the gold Tagus;
[Caesar took all the gold from the Hispanias...]

nunc Galliae timetur et Britanniae.
now he fears for Gaul and for Britannia.

quid hunc malum fovetis? aut quid hic potest
Why do you protect this wicked? What can he do

nisi uncta devour heritage?
this more than devour fat patrimonies?

eone nomine urbis opulentissime,
And with those credentials, owners and lords of the city,

socer generque, perdidistis omnia?
father-in-law and son-in-law, have you spoiled everything?

LVII.
ad Gaium Iulium Caesarem
Pulcre convenit improbis cinaedis,
It goes great for those evil homosexuals:

Mamurrae pathicoque Caesarique.
Mamurra's penis sucker and (Julius) Caesar.

nec mirum: maculae pares utrisque,
And it's not strange: both with the same spots,
urbana altera et illa Formiana,
some in Rome, others in Formias,

impressae resident nec eluentur:
recorded are kept and will not be erased;

morbosi pariter, gemelli utrique,
sick alike, both like twins,

uno in lecticulo erudituli ambo,
in a single little bed taught both,

non hic quam ille magis vorax adulter,

not (is) this one more voracious adulterer than that one,

rivales socii puellularum*.
even rival partners for young girls.
* The poet Catullus accuses Julius Caesar of having sex with minors.

pulcre convenit improbis cinaedis.
Those wicked homosexuals are doing great.

ORAL SEX

Oral sex was always totally rejected, although the most acceptable for Roman sexual morality was the one performed with slaves, prostitutes or between men.

Fellatio was a censored and despised practice, as well as in anal sex between two men, being penetrated.
With women it could be used as a contraceptive measure, especially with girls from noble families, instead of withdrawing before ejaculating, the only known contraceptive methods.
It is said that Julia, daughter of Emperor Augustus, had sexual relations outside of marriage while she was pregnant with her husband, so she avoided unwanted pregnancies. Augustus disinherited her and sentenced her and her granddaughter to exile.

The most degrading action for the man was to perform oral sex on a woman **(cunnilingus),** who was accused of it, even if it was false, he was crossed out with a note of infamy, which meant that he could not vote, inherit or defend himself in court, remaining in the same social position as gladiators, pimps or ruffians, poststitutes and actors.

Suburban Baths, Pompeii. Apodyterium, scene IV.

The formal loss of good reputation (**fame**) was carried out by the censors, defenders of public morals.

Martial, Epigrams.
XL
Tarpeias Diodorus ad coronas
When Diodorus, at the Tarpeya contest,

Romam cum peteret Pharo relicta,
To Rome he went, having left Faros,

vovit pro reditu viri Philaenis
she made a vow, for the return of her husband, Filenis

illam lingeret ut puella simplex

to suck him like a simple girl

quam castae quoque diligunt Sabinae.
that which even the Sabine castes seek.

dispersa rate tristibus procellis,
The ship dilapidated by a fatal storm,

mersus fluctibus obrutusque ponto,
submerged in the waves and broken by the sea,

ad votum Diodorus enatavit.
in search of the vote, Diodorus, swam out.

O tardus nimis et piger maritus!
Oh, too late and lazy husband!

hoc in litore si puella votum,
If my beloved a similar vote on the coast,

fecisset mea, protinus redissem.
I would have done, I would have gone back without wasting
time.

Catullus
LXXVIIIb.
sed nunc id doleo, quod purae pura puellae.
But now this I regret: that you are a pure girl.

suavia comminxit spurca saliva tua.
the kisses your obscene saliva will piss.

(verum) id non impune feres: (nam) te omnia saecla.

But that will not go unpunished: for all the centuries.

noscent et, qui sis, fame loquetur anus.
They will know you and the old fame will tell what kind of
man you are.

In this poem Catullus attacks all those men who interfered
in the relationship with his beloved Lesbia, using oral sex as
a weapon of denigration and submission.

Tavern Pimps

XXXVII.
Ad contubernales et Egnatium

Salax tavern vosque contubernales,
Lascivious tavern, and you, his companions,

to Pilleatis Nona Fratribus Pila,
the one of the ninth column after the brothers of the pileus*,
*pileus, hat used by the slaves who achieved their freedom
and that all citizens used in the Saturnalia festivities.

solis putatis esse mentulas vobis,
Do you think that you only have a penis,

solis licere, quidquid est puellarum, [confutuere]*
that only you are allowed to do it with all the girls

[*] et putare ceteros hircos?
  and consider the others cuckolds?

(an), continenter (quod) sedetis insulsi
(Or), (because) you are sitting one after the other like idiots

centum an ducenti, non putatis ausurum
a hundred or two hundred, do you think I will not dare

me a ducentos irrumare sessores?
at once to the two hundred spectators to fill your mouth?
(he alludes to everyone performing oral sex on him).

atqui putate: namque totius vobis
Well, believe it: because (with) all of you

frontem tabernae sopionibus scribam.
In front of the tavern I will inscribe.

puella nam mi, quae meo sinu fugit,
Well, my girl, who has fled from my arms,

amata tantum quantum amabitur nulla,
whom I love as much as no one will love anyone,

pro qua mihi sunt magna bella pugnata,
for which I have fought great wars,

consedit istic. hanc boni beatique,
she sits there. You all love her, so honored and happy,

omnes amatis, et quidem, quod indignum est,
but, of course, what a shame!

omnes pusilli et semitarii moechi;
you all (are) some miserable lovers of dark alley;

SEXUAL POSTURES IN ART

The sexual posture that is most represented in iconography
is "a tergo" (from behind), in which the man is usually
standing and the woman is bent or kneeling. It must have
been the most common for different reasons:
•It does not require the use of furniture: beds, beds... not
even being
  inside the house.
•It is the natural position in which mammals copulate.
•The position of the homoxesual copula.
  In some cases it also represents anal sex between a man
and a woman.
•The one that occurs between the master and slave or slave
(submission)
•Expresses a certain distance with the woman and lack of
attachment or affection in the act.
On Greek amphorae the woman is shown resting her hands
on a chair or stool while she is possessed from behind her.
Lysistrata in the oath for sexual abstinence:
"No man will come near me... At home I will spend my life
chastely dressed in saffron (just as newlyweds go) and well
groomed so that my husband can't wait for me.
I will never give in willingly to do so and if he were to
compel me by force, I will reluctantly surrender and not
move or raise my feet to the ceiling or get on top of his
belly...".
**The only posture that remains to be mentioned is that of a
tergo or back.**

Other sexual positions that appear in mosaics and ceramic pieces, represent a totally naked woman or with a bra and a man kneeling on the bed or standing who supports one or both legs of his partner on his shoulder.
The woman sitting on the man facing or placed in the opposite direction to her partner.
Representations of oral sex and anal sex practiced by two mens.

Scenes from erotic
paintings. Pompeii.

The painted Latin inscription reads: LE(NT)E IMPELLE, Push slowly.

The Greek ideal of male beauty is described by
Aristophanes: "strong chest, white skin, broad shoulders,
short tongue, big ass, small penis."
The large penis is contrary to beauty and belongs to old
men, barbarians or fabulous beings.

Martial. Epigrams.

47
Subdola famee moneo fuge
from the nets of a famous adulteress, I advise you, run
away

retia moechae, leuior or conchis, Galle, Cytheriacis.
oh Gaul, why more hairless than the shells of Cythera?

Confidis natibus?
Do you trust your buttocks?

Non est pedico maritus;
The husband does not have anal sex;

quae faciat duo sunt: irrumat aut futuit.
he does it in two (ways), either through the mouth or
through the vagina.

Ovid says about it in Remedio Amoris

Remedy Amoris. Sexual postures

Et pudet, et dicam: venerem quoque iunge figura,
It makes me blush, but I'll say it: in your passionate
struggles,

Qua minime iungi quamque decere potas.
choose the position that you think is less favorable to your
friend.

Nec labor efficere est: frase sibi vera fatentur,
The thing is not difficult; few confess to themselves the
truth,

Et nihil est, quod se dedecuisse putent.
and recognize any mole in its beauty.

Tunc etiam iubeo totas aperire fenestras,
So, I command you, open all the windows,

Turpiaque admisso membra notare die.
and in full light she contemplates the blemishes on her
body.

Lassaque cum tota corpora iacent mind,
and your body and your soul fall from lassitude,

Dum piget, et malis nullam tetigisse puellam,
so much that, full of boredom, you wish you had never
touched any woman,

Tacturusque tibi non videare diu,
and promise yourself not to touch her for a long time,

Quid, qui clam latuit reddente obscene puella,
What shall I say of the one who hides and surprises her
beloved at the moment of relieving her,

Et vidit, quae mos ipse videre vetat?
and sees what decency has always forbidden to be seen?

Di melius, quam nos moneamus talia quemquam!
The gods do not want us to advise anyone of this audacity;
Ut prosint, non sunt expedienda tamen.
such resources, although helpful, should not be put into
practice;

Eros et Psique.Villa Romana of Casale.Sicilian

It was frowned upon for women to have sex completely naked, which is why prostitutes wore bras that they did not usually take off during sexual activity.

Centennial house, Pompeii.

He man lying down and the woman wearing a fascia pectoralis or strophium (bra), with her hand seems to stimulate the male's genitals...

Lupanar.Painting of a couple making love with the woman in the position of cowgirl.
She has her breasts covered by a cloth band or bra (fascia pectoralis), something that is very common in artistic representations.

The breasts did not have any erotic connotation, that is why they were covered while the sexual act was taking place. Pubic hair was shaved by teenage girls and married women as a hygienic but not aesthetic measure, much like trimming nails.

Prostitutes used pubic hair as another adornment:
They shaved it, dyed it, or put on a hairpiece of pubic hair in blonder colors.

Pubic hair removal was common in ancient times, for aesthetic and hygiene reasons(oral sex).

Egyptian women completely depilated their bodies with a mixture of sugar, water, lemon and cucumber (**sugar wax**) or with oil and honey, which was allowed to dry.

In Ancient Greece, the removal of pubic hair represented a sign of youth and beauty. For this they used candles with which they burned the hair or rubbed with a pumice stone. The hetairas used a depilatory cream (**dropax**), made of vinegar and a very fine mud.

The Romans used a kind of tar or pitch (**philotrum**).

Suburban baths.Pompeii.Apodyterium.Scene I.

Vessels and personal care objects were found in the Pompeii brothel, as well as some rudimentary razor blades to shave one's own hair and that of clients, even for hairdressing jobs.

Hair removal

Martial.Epigrams
6.56
Quod tibi crura rigent saetis et pectora uillis,
Because (you have) your legs bristling with bristles and your chest with hair,

uerba whores fame you, Charideme, dare.
Do you think, Caridemo, that you can cheat fame?.

Extirpa, mihi crede, pilos de corpore toto
Remove, believe me, the hairs from all over your body

teque pilare tuas testificare natis.
and give us proof that you have shaved your buttocks.

"Quae ratio est?" inquis.
"What's the reason?" you ask.

Scis multos dicere multa:
You know that many say many things:

fac pedicari te, Charideme, putent.
Make them think, Caridemo, that you put your ass.

62
Quod pectus, quod crura tibi, quod bracchia uellis,
If you shave your chest, legs and arms,

quod cincta est breuibus mentula tonsa pilis,
and if surrounded by short hairs, your shaved cock is

hoc praestas, Labiene, tuae, quis nescit?, amicae.
you do this, Labienus, who does not know?, in attention to
your friend.

Cui praestas, culum quod, Labiene, pilas?
If you shave your ass, Labienus, who are you doing it for?

74
Psilothro faciem leuas et dropace caluam:
You wax your face with ointments and your bald spot with
concoctions:

numquid tonsorem, Gargiliane, times?
Are you so afraid, Gargiliano, of the barber?

Quid facient ungues?
What will your nails do?

Nam certe non potes illos resina Veneto nec resecare luto.
Because you certainly cannot cut them with resin, nor with
mud from the Veneto.

Desine, si pudor est, miseram traducere caluam:
If you have any shame, stop making a show of your head.

hoc fieri cunno, Gargiliane, solet.
This with the pussy, Gargiliano, is usually done,

UNDERWEAR

Underwear (**indumenta**) began to be worn during the Republic.

Unmarried daughters of noble citizens used to wear the **toga praetexta** until puberty or marriage, when they wore the stola (long-sleeved full-length tunic).

Prostitutes (**metretrix meretricis meretrices**) and women divorced for adultery were required to wear the toga of motherhood (toga muliebris).

Indusium or Subucula (subuculae)

Very light inner tunic that reached the feet, made up of two pieces of cloth that were sewn together to form a single piece.
Made without sleeves or with short or long sleeves, of wool, linen, cotton or silk [thick fabric (spissa) or fine (ralla or rare)], almost transparent and without a belt, very light, it was used by women as underwear , under other clothes, or to sleep.

Camisia(Shirt)

Of Gallic origin, it was similar to the subucula, shorter and with sleeves, used by men. Its simplicity and comfort made it very popular in the army.

Under the **subucula** they wore:

Fascia and strophium(strophia)

The fascia pectoralis or strophium, is a rectangular band or strip of fabric or leather that covered and supported the woman's breasts, similar to an English bra.

Used by young women when their bust began to grow, it comes from **fasces** (or bunch of tied rods carried by the lictors, or assistants of the Consuls).

The strophium was used as a bag.
In Great Britain, remains of underwear with anatomical cut and leather straps to be adjusted, similar to bikinis, were found.

The first bikinis of the history

Durius incident? fac inambulet; omne papillae
if she walks without panache, invite her to move, and if her
excessively voluminous glands

Pectus habent? vitium fascia nulla tegat.
They cover his chest, take off the girdle that hides them
from you.
Ovid. Remedy Amoris.

The mamillare (mamillaria)

The **mamillare**, made of leather strips, similar to the bodice,
in addition to holding, flattened.

"They dress in veils that pass for clothes as if to excuse
their apparent nudity. But the interior can be seen more
clearly than their faces, except for their breasts, which are
always tied up like prisoners."
(Lucian.Loves).

Subligar subligara subligaculum (from subligo, to tie underneath)

Rectangular wool garment worn to cover their genitals and
belly.
It was a unique garment for work or sports, very common
among slaves, agricultural or manual workers and
gladiators, used by both men and women.

The **subligaculum subligacula** was longer than the subligacula, and was held up by a belt (cintus).

SEX TOYS.

In ancient Greece there were already dildos or dildos, called by Aristophanes in his work, Lysistrata: Olisbos or widows' dildos.

Of different sizes, they had the shape of a male phallus. Made on a wooden base, they were covered with leather or animal skin. Those made of finely polished dog skin, which slid easily, were the most appreciated. They were lubricated with olive oil or melted animal fat and have eight finger (15 cms, simple dildos or with added testicles).

Lysistrata. Not even of those peculiar lovers have we had anything since the Milesians betrayed us: I have not seen a single eight-finger-long leather dildo that will give us any relief. So if I found a way, would you end the war with my help?.

The leather dildo (olisbos) was made in Miletus, Asia Minor, present-day Turkey.

After the defeat in Sicily, when Miletus departs from the military alliance with Athens, they are no longer sold in other Greek cities.

The most appreciated dildos were made of dog skin, which is why Aristophanes plays with the double meaning of Kyon in Greek: dog and penis.

Lysistrata. I will tell you, because there is no point in continuing to hide the matter. Women, if we are going to force men to make peace, we have to refrain from... Are you going to do it?.

Cleonice. We will, even if we have to die.

Lysistrata. Well, we have to refrain from the penis.

Cleonice. I won't be able to: I prefer war...

Lysistrata. Lost is our gender, that's why tragedies are made at our expense, because they only taught us to do it and to give birth.

Cleonice. But what will happen if our husbands leave us?.

Lysistrata. We will do as Ferecrates: we will skin a dog.

Cleonice. Those substitutes don't work for me, besides, what if the husband drags us by force to the bedroom?.

Lysistrata. You, hold on to the door... make it difficult for him, cause him pain, let him take no pleasure in such things... he will quit. Well, the man will never enjoy if he does not agree with the woman.

-There is no historical source that states that Cleopatra queen used a box full of bees to sexually stimulate her genitals.

-Regarding Cleopatra performing oral sex on Roman soldiers, there is a misrepresentation of Plutarch's historical source in their parallel lives where what is really expressed about the empress is only the following:

"She possessed an infinite voluptuousness when speaking, and so much sweetness and harmony in the sound of her voice that her tongue was like a multi-stringed instrument that she handled easily and that she extracted, as she well suited her, the most delicate nuances of her language. Plato recognizes four kinds of flattery, but she had a thousand."

In Ancient Egypt, oral sex had a sacred value. Osiris was brought back to life when Isis performed fellatio on a clay penis.

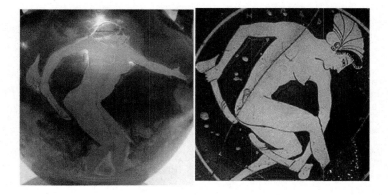

Greek vase from the 5th century BC, woman using a dildo (olisbos).

In the Satyricon of Petronius, Encolpio, losing his sexual vigor, resorts to the services of a priestess who wants to apply a curious remedy: being penetrated with a dildo and whipped with nettle branches.

Herodas (3rd century BC), a Greek author in a humorous way:

Metro: Don't fool me, dear Koritto, who was it that sewed you the black dildo?.

Koritto: You'll leave me in a bad place if I tell you.

Metro: I swear to you, no one will listen to what you say.

Koritto: Eubule gave it to me and begged me not to say a word.

Metro: I took pity on him because he kept begging me, and I gave him [the dildo], before using it myself! .

And she, as if it were something of little value, grabs it and gives it to the wrong person, even if he had a thousand dildos, he wouldn't give her even one, even if it were rough!.

What shoemaker has sewn it?.

Koritto: The shoemaker Kerdón sewed it. He works at home, selling under the table, as you well know. He went to see me and brought two, and when I saw them my eyes widened with desire: men don't have penises so erect! And also you don't know how soft they are... they have the softness and sweetness of sleep! And the ribbons are wool.

Lucianus in his work Amores de él, complains about the use of a double dildo by two women:

"That they submit to the artifice of lascivious instruments. It is a sterile monstrosity that a woman has sex with another woman as if she were a man".

Suburban Baths.Pompeii.Apdyterium, scene II.

ADULTERY

Adultery, or sexual intercourse between married persons outside of marriage, was punishable by fines and loss of property: confiscation by the State of half of the property of the adulterous man, one third of the property of the woman and half of her dowry and the right of the spouse to repudiate the adulterer (**Divortium ex iusta causa**).

Julius Caesar's infidelities. Relationship with Cleopatra.

In Life of the Twelve Caesars, Suetonius narrates the following:

LII.
Dilexit et reginas;
He also had affairs with queens,

sed maxime Cleopatram,
but the one he loved most was Cleopatra,

cum qua et convivia in primam lucem saepe protraxit
with which you feast until dawn frequently prolonged

et eadem nave thalamego paene Aethiopia tenus Aegyptum penetravit,
and in a sumptuously rigged ship from Egypt to Ethiopia

she would have gone into them,

nisi exercitus sequi recusasset,
if the army had not refused to follow him.

He made her come to Rome, showering her with gifts
...
appellare nomine suo passus est.
and that her name (the son she had by her) bear her name,
having consented to it.

Quem quidem nonnulli Graecorum similem quoque Caesari
et forma et incessu tradiderunt.
Some Greek writers said that he (this son) resembled
Caesar in face and bearing.

M. Antonius adgnitum etiam ab eo senatui adfirmavit,
M. Antony who had recognized him (Caesar), in full Senate
assured,

quae scire C. Matium et C. Oppium reliquosque Caesaris
amicos;
he invoked the testimony of C. Matio, C. Oppio and other
friends of Caesar;
*Note. Once Caesar had died, to weaken the position of
Octavian, Caesar's nephew and adopted son and his sole
heir.

quorum Gaius Oppius, quasi plane defensione ac patronage
res egeret, librum editit,
But C. Oppio rejected such an assertion by publishing a
book entitled:

non esse Caesaris filium, quem Cleopatra dicat.
It is not the son of Caesar who Cleopatra claims to be.

The tribune of the plebs Cinna declares...

(tr. pl.)* plerisque confessus est habuisse se scriptam paratamque legem,
... to many people he stated that he had drafted and prepared a law,
*tribune of the plebs.

quam Caesar ferre iussisset cum ipse abesset,
that Caesar propose commanded him in his absence,

uti [uxores] liberorum [quaerendorum* causa quas et quot uellet ducere] (liceret).
by which he (was allowed) [to marry as many women as he wanted] in order to have children.

At ne cui dubium omnino sit et impudicitiae et adulteriorum flagrasse infamia,
in short, their customs were so disordered and their adulteries so ostensible the infamy,

Curio pater quadam eum oratione appellat.
that Curio father in a speech calls him.

omnium mulierum virum et omnium virorum mulierem,
of all women, husband and of all husbands, wife,
* Referring to his bisexual orientation.

Joyful life of Julius Caesar during the Gallic Wars.

His own legionnaires warn him in the songs with which they celebrate his triumphal entry into Rome.

LI.
Urbani, servate uxores, moechum calvum adducimus
Citizens, hide your wives, that we bring to the bald adulterer;
*Note.César was bald, which he tried to hide by wearing toupees.

Aurum in Gallia effutuisti, at hic*(adverb)sumpsisti mutuum.
with the gold in Gaul you fornicated that here* you borrowed [stolen from the Romans].

Accusations of adultery made by Marcus Antonius.

M. Antonius super festinatas Liviae nuptias obiecit et feminam consularem
M. Antony, even accuses him that in a feast to the wife of a consular,

e triclinium viri coram in cubiculum abductam,
from the banquet table to an adjoining room, the husband being present, he ushered in,

rursus in convivium rubentibus auriculis incomptiore capillo reductam;
and again at the banquet with red ears and disheveled hair;

dimissam Scriboniam, quia liberius doluisset nimiam potentiam paelicis;
he disowned Scribonia because he more freely regretted

the excessive influence of a concubine.
*paelex paelicis, concubine.

(condiciones) quaesitas per amicos,
that his friends were looking for him,

Qui matres familias et adultas aetate virgines denudarent
married women and nubile maidens who had to manifest
certain (condiciones),

atque perspicerent, tamquam mangone vendente.
and he examined them as slaves for sale in the market.

Scribit etiam ad ipsum haec familiariter adhuc necdum
plane inimicus aut hostis:
At a time when he was not yet his declared enemy,
[Antonius] wrote to him familiarly:

"Quid te mutavit? Quod reginam ineo? Uxor mea est. Nunc
coepi an abhinc annos novem?
What has changed you? Let my lover be a queen? She is my
wife,
and not yesterday, but already nine years ago.

Tu deinde solam Liviam inis?
Do you only have Livia?

Ita valeas, uti tu, hanc epistulam cum leges,
I am sure that by the time you read my letter,

non inieris ... aut omnes.
you will have already enjoyed ..., or perhaps all of them.

Martial, Epigrams.

Homosexual adultery

90

Quod numquam maribus iunctam te, Bassa, uidebam

Since I never saw you hang out with men, Basa,

quodque tibi moechum fabula nulla dabat,

and because no rumor a lover attributed to you,

omne sed officium circa te semper obibat turba tui sexus,
non adeunte uiro,

but that around you you always had at your service a group
of your own sex, without the presence of a man,

esse uidebaris, fateor, Lucretia nobis:

It seemed to me that you were, I confess, a Lucrezia.

at tu, pro facinus, Bassa, fututor eras.

But you, Basa, what an atrocity! You did it like a man.

Inter se geminos audes committere cunnos mentiturque
uirum prodigiosa Venus.

You dare to unite twin pussies with each other and your
huge clitoris does like the man.

Commenta es dignum Thebano aenigmate monstrum,

Monstrous idea worthy of the Theban riddle:

* enigma of the sphinx that no one knew how to decipher..

hic ubi uir non est, ut sit adulterium.

that, here where there is no man, there is adultery.

Marcial wonders if there is infidelity (adultery) of the wife who has a homosexual relationship with another woman.

Catullus. Adultery. ad Gallum

LXXVIII.

Gallus habet fratres, quorum est lepidissima coniunx
Galo has two brothers, one of whom has a very attractive wife,

alterius, lepidus filius alterius.
the other an attractive son.

Gallus homo est bellus: nam sweet iungit loves,
Galo is a beautiful man, because he unites sweet loves,

cum puero ut bello bella puella cubet.
I made the beautiful girl beautiful.

Gallus homo est stultus, nec se videt esse maritum,
Galo is an idiot, and he doesn't realize that he is a married man,

qui patruus patrui monstret adulterium.
who, as a man, teaches adultery thanks to a man.

Juvenal.Satires.Infidelities of the wife

Juvenal tells us about the infidelity of the newly married woman.

Note. For the historical doctrine, the misogyny of this Latin author is manifest.

ornatas paulo ante fores,
adorned shortly before the doors,

pendentia linquit uela domus
the hanging veils of the house abandon

et adhuc uirides in limine ramos.
and still the green branches on the lintel.

(sic) crescit numerus, (sic) fiunt octo mariti quinque per autumnos,
This is how the number of husbands grows, eight arrive in five autumns (5 years):

titulo res digna sepulcri.
matter worthy of an epitaph.

Desperanda tibi salua concordia socru.
Despairing of harmony while your mother-in-law is healthy.

illa docet spoliis nudi gaudere mariti,
She teaches him to enjoy the remains of the poor husband,

decipit illa custodes aut aere domat.
and she was the one to deceive the guards or subdue them with money.

illa docet missis a corruptore tabellis nil rude nec simplex

rescribet shows him sent by the corrupter the note, neither
elementary nor simple, to cheat

tum corpore sana aduocat Archigenen onerosaque pallia
iactat.
afterwards (when) the body is healthy he calls Arguigenes
and throws heavy blankets.

Abditus interea latet et secretus, adulter
Hidden, meanwhile, hidden and secretly the lover

inpatiensque morae silet et praeputia ducit.
and impatient to wait, he is silent and her foreskin prepares.

scilicet expectations ut tradat mater
Do you by any chance expect this mother to transmit

honest atque alios mores quam quos habet?
other good habits to which she has her?

PROSTITUTION

The Greek historian Herodotus tells us about the
prostitution carried out in Babylon as an offering to the
goddess Ishtar:
The lowest of Babylonian customs is the one that compels
every woman in that land to go to the temple of Aphrodite
and sleep with a stranger at least once in her life...Great
crowds of women come and go in rows that they run in all
directions, through which men circulate and choose.
Once the woman arrives at the temple, she does not go
home until some man puts some coins on her lap and lies
with her outside the temple... the woman cannot refuse, for

to do so would be a sin, and she offers that money to the goddess
After she has sex, she is free from that sacred obligation and goes to her house, that happens quickly with the most beautiful women, while the ugly ones must wait to comply with the law; some of them stay that way for many years.
In Greece something similar was done in the city of Corinth in the temple of Aphrodite, goddess of
sexuality, which housed thousands of courtesans (heteras). According to Strabo, foreigners visited Corinth attracted by this activity, something in which they spent a large amount of money, for which a proverb remained: traveling to Corinth is not within everyone's reach.

The **fornix fornices** ("brothels") derived from the word arch or vault (because it was under the arches of the buildings where this activity was carried out) were identified by a stone phallus, a representation of Priapus, god of sexual vigor and fertility, painted vermilion red; a penis carved in stone, where it is written: hic habitat felicitat, happiness lives here; or a brothel with a goblet for the game of dice, placed above the door knocker.

In Pompeii with a population of about 10,000 inhabitants there were 9 brothels.
In an inscription on one of the walls of the basilica can be read:
If someone is looking for sweet love in this city, the girls here are very friendly.

The prostitutes could not wear a veil, a symbol of purity, they wore short brightly colored tunics, wore wigs or dyed blonde hair.

they wore wigs or dyed blonde hair, bras on their chests without panties on their private parts.
The laws forced them to put on a female toga so that anyone could easily distinguish them (**toga muliebris**).

They covered her face with a thick layer of makeup, rouge on her cheeks, charcoal on her eyes, gold glitter nipples, her pubis completely shaved, and her vaginal lips dyed vermilion red.
From the 1st century B.C. They used to shave their entire bodies. The pubic hair was completely removed.
They chewed mastic leaves to prevent bad breath.
On the soles of the shoes they engraved the words: sequere me (follow me) that was drawn in the dust and indicated to customers where to find them.

Cato, the Censor, in the 2nd century BC, a staunch defender of Roman virtue and morality, saw favorably that the citizen would visit brothels, so that his base desires could damage the modesty of free women.

Each position had a specific price that varied according to the education, age and physical appearance of the male or female prostitute.

On the walls of Pompeii, we can see some of these inscriptions used as propaganda to attract customers.
The price for oral sex varied between one and two aces:
Felix sucks for 1 as.

Lais sucks for 2 ases.

Mauricius licks her pussy for 4 ases.He is also ready to service virgin girls.

The price for any other service (vaginal or anal) varied

between 2 and 16 ases.

At the end of the Republic, Clodia, lover of the poet Catullus, was accused by another of her lovers of trying to poison him, who, during the trial, came to call her quadrantaria, (a prostitute who charged 1/4 as for her service).

Inflation pushed these prices up to 1 or 2 ases during the empire, as Pompeii shows, but the real value remained very low (Pompeii was destroyed by the eruption of Vesuvius in AD 79).

According to Juvenal, 1 quadrant, (quadrans quadrantis) 1/4 of an as, was the price of a bath in the public baths:

caedere Siluano porcum, quadrante lauari.

immolate a pig to Silvano and take a bath for a quadrant

An educated slave was paid 2 ases, the price of a cheap glass of wine.

Felicula, slave of good upbringing, she does it for 2 ases.

Pitane salutes you, I do it for 3 three bronze ases.

Parte, nice girl does it for 6 ases.

With the house slave, 8 ases.

If anyone sits here, please know that Attica draws 16 ases.

Harpocras did it here with Drauca for a silver denarius

IV

Aureolis futui cum possit Galla duobus

Being able to sleep with Gala for two gold coins

et plus quam futui, si totidem addideris:

and more than going to bed, if another amount is added
(2+2= 4 coins),

aureolos a te cur accipit, Aeschyle, give us?

Why does he charge you, Aeschylus, ten?

non fellat tanti Galla. Quid ergo? Tacet.
For sucking it, Gala does not charge so much. Why then? to shut up
Martial.Epigrams.

Preliminary games were not to Roman taste, it can be read in one of these graffiti found on the walls of a Pompeian brothel:
I arrived, I did it and I went home quickly.
In group sex you could get to pay 5 aces per person.
If they requested the service of two girls, they were paid a somewhat higher price than each one separately,
Athenais, 2 bronze ases. Sabina, 2 bronze aces. We both do it for Two and a half ases.
A full night cost between 48 and 60 bronze aces.

The **hetairas, heteras** or courtesans did not charge a certain price because their clients considered themselves lovers. They received for their intellectual, artistic and/or sexual services, different gifts, food, clothes, jewelry, house rent or some money.
Not all the rich young people paid with money for the services received, but some tried to pay with their beauty, something underestimated by the courtesans, for which they preferred to associate with older men or physically unattractive.
Most of these heteras, slave prostitutes or courtesans, had to carry out this activity for most of their lives. Some managed to buy their freedom: "Telesina, well known among the women of the Suburra, won her freedom at the cost of her body... ".

The prostitutes were usually women who had been subjected to slavery: foreigners who were part of the spoils of war of the Roman legions, girls abandoned (exposita) by their own father (pater familia) at birth or sold by him to the highest bidder if so. wanted, something that aberrant in our eyes, was legal for the oldest Roman Law.

Those in the best condition had the status of free women, manumitted by their former owners.

In the Roman double standard, the prostitute was rejected and considered turpis or a person incapable of holding rights, as were actors, actresses, dancers, musicians, and gladiators.

Curiously, those who did not have any citizen rights, did have to pay taxes to the State for carrying out their activity, register in the census of the city of Rome, in addition to dressing differently from married women or matrons (wearing the toga muliebris, as well as women convicted of adultery).

The famous dancers of Cádiz (**puella gaditanae, or cinaedi** if they were boys), who with the sway of their hips, aroused desire, as well as the flutists or zither players, did not have to carry out another type of activity with the clients, although in some cases they did.

The prostitutes belonged to a **leno**, (ruffian or pimp) who exploited them without the slightest consideration or humanity.

This pimp ran a brothel or brothel, as described in Plautus's comedy, Pseudolus, where a young man from a good family falls in love with Phoenicia and tries to get her out of that harsh and cruel life in the hands of the ruffian Balion. Misunderstandings, and the help of Pseudolus, rogue and faithful slave of the young man, lead to a happy outcome,

outwitting the ruffian who intended to make a great deal.
The pimp gave the client a card with the name of the girl,
the room (**cella**) where he was and the sexual practice to be
carried out, which was as brief as possible to increase the
economic benefits of the sexual exploiter.
On the wall of a brothel in Pompeii can be read:
"As soon as I got here, I fucked up and quickly went home."

Those men who practiced prostitution did not have the **ius
defendiendi**
or right to defend themselves, nor could they access the
magistracies.
If they were marked as infamous, they could be beaten,
mutilated or raped with impunity.
The note of infamy that a censor carried out was a legal
stigma for life: the formal loss of good reputation or fame,
for having carried out shameful behavior, such as
prostitution.
Remember that Cato was a censor.

The pimps were also branded as infamous. They were the
men who obtained some economic benefit from the sexual
activity of a woman, who could even be her own wife. The
Leges Juliae, punished the husband who obtained
economic gain with the adultery of his own wife.

In this epigram Marcial says:
Vxorem, Charideme, tuam scis ipse sinisque a medico futui:
To your wife, Caridemo, you know and consent that I do it
with a doctor:

uis sine febre mori.

you want to die without fever

Until the arrival of Augustus and his more conservative morals, the open practice of prostitution was tolerated. He passed strict laws against adultery, celibacy (or singleness) and disorderly conduct.
The most common terms used to address women who engaged in prostitution were **lupa** or she-wolf*, **meretrix, moecha, puella, scortum, scortillum.**
Amica is the most common word, for example, it appears in Plautus's Pseudolus.
* Titus Livy, in his work Ab urbe condita, tells the story of Romulus and Remus.
The children are found by a wealthy rancher and cared for by his wife Acca Larentia. The belief that they were suckled by a she-wolf could have come from the fact that Acca could have carried out this activity, since that is what prostitutes were called in Latin.

Tenet fame cum fluitantem alveum, quo expositi erat pueri, tenuis in sicco aqua destituisset,
Tradition goes on to say that after the floating cradle, in which the children had been abandoned,

eam submissas infantibus adeo mitem praebuisse mammas ut lingua lambentem pueros,
she would have been carried to dry land by the receding waters,

lupam sitientem ex montibus qui circa sunt ad puerilem vagitum cursum flexisse;
a thirsty she-wolf, from the nearby mountains, and attracted by the crying of the children went down,

a thirsty she-wolf from the surrounding hills, drawn by the crying children, approached them,

eam submissas infantibus adeo mitem praebuisse mammas,
tamed to such an extent that the children began to breastfeed, she nursed them and was so sweet to them,

ut lingua lambentem pueros,
her while she licked the children with her tongue,
that she licking the children with her tongue,

magister regii pecoris invenerit,
The chief shepherd of the king's flocks found them,
a shepherd of the king found her.

Faustulus fuisse nomen, ferunt,
They say that his name was Faustulus,
According to the story, the shepherd's name was Faustus.

ab eo ad stabula Larentiae uxori educando datos.
It is said that he took the children to his house and gave them to his wife Larentia to raise.
He took the children to his hut and gave them to his wife Larentia to raise.

Sunt* qui Larentiam volgato corpore lupam inter pastores vocatam putent;
There are those who believe that this Larentia prostituted her body and (for this reason) among the shepherds she was called she-wolf (prostitute).
Some authors think that Larentia, because she had prostituted her body, was called "She-wolf" among the

shepherds,

inde locum fabulae ac miraculo datum.
and from here comes this wonderful tradition.
and that this was the origin of the wonderful story.

MESALINE

Messalina, daughter of Valerius Mesala Barbatus and
Domicia, niece of
Augustus's sister, only 15 years old, becomes the third wife
of Claudius, who is already 50 years old (a few months later,
he is acclaimed emperor).

Messalina has two children by Claudius: **Octavia and
Britanic**.
The emperor is unconcerned about his wife, occupying all
her time with bureaucratic tasks.

According to the geographer Pliny the Elder, while Emperor
Claudius was on campaign in Britannia, Messalina took
advantage of his absence, and organized a sexual
competition with the prostitutes of Rome and some women
of the nobility, which took place in the imperial palace, to
find out. who of all those women can sleep with more men
in one night.

In the end, only Messalina herself and a prostitute named
Scylla (monster that shipwrecked sailors in the Strait of
Messina) remained, but she could not be with more than 25
men, while Messalina, having already been with 70 men,
continued until sleeping with 200.
The prostitute said: "This unfortunate woman has an iron

sex of hers."

According to the poet Juvenal, Messalina dresses as a prostitute and leaves the palace at dawn to prostitute herself in the Subura neighborhood under the Greek nickname of **Lycisca**, which in Greek means she-wolf, (nickname of prostitute).
Historians do not agree: according to Tacitus, Flavius Josephus and Tenth Juvenal she habitually prostituted herself, while for Dio Cassius she did so occasionally.

Tenth June Juvenal narrates that "as soon as she believed that her husband was asleep, this imperial prostitute put on the cape she wore at night and left the house accompanied by a slave, since she preferred a cheap bed to the royal bed... her black hair with a blonde wig and she would go to the lupanar of worn upholstery, where she had reserved a camera. Then she would take her place, totally naked and with her nipples painted in gold bread, she called herself Lyscisca...".

Messalina married her lover, Gaius Silius, committing the crime of bigamy and plans to assassinate the emperor. The imperial secretary, Narciso, finds out about the conspiracy, warns Cláudio who orders the suicide of his wife.
Finally, a soldier from her guard kills her by cutting off his head with her sword.
Claudio was never aware of his wife's activities.
Her weak memory was used by Messalina for her purposes, making her believe that he had ordered something from her, that she made him sign.
He did not remember that he had ordered the death of his wife and found out about it because she was surprised that

she did not go down to dinner with him.
Claudius ordered that all statues of Messalina be removed from public and private places.

Couple in bed.House of Caecilius Iucundis, Pompeii.

JUVENAL SATIRE

Looking for a good wife

conuentum tamen et pactum et sponsalia nostra
tempestate paras
However, in our time, the ceremony, the contract and the
betrothal you prepare;

iamque a tonsore magistro pecteris et digito pignus
fortasse dedisti?
Already for the master hairdresser you comb your hair and
perhaps on the finger the garment you gave
(He refers to the fact that the value of the ring is the wife's
greatest guarantee of fidelity, since she would lose it in
case of divorce).

certe sanus eras. uxorem, Postume, ducis?
Surely you were sane, and wife do you take, Postumus?

aut si de multis nullus placet (exitus),
or if of many (outings) none pleases you,

illud nonne putas melius, quod tecum pusio dormit?
Don't you think it's better for a boy to sleep with you?

sed placet Vrsidio lex Iulia: tollere dulcem cogitat heredem,
But Ursidio likes the Julia law: in raising a sweet heir he
thinks

cariturus turture magno
on condition of depriving oneself of a good turtle dove

pusio, qui noctu non litigat,
A young man who does not quarrel at night,

exigit a te nulla iacens illic munuscula,
that he does not demand any small gift from you by
sleeping with him.
(when you sleep with him).

nec queritur quod et lateri parcas
and don't complain that you give your kidneys a rest

nec quantum iussit desires.
and do not yearn for his orders.

quid quod et antiquis uxor de moribus illi quaeritur?
What if I told you that he was looking for a wife of ancient
customs?
And what to say that he is looking for a wife of ancient
customs

or medici, nimiam pertundite uenam.
Oh doctors, she goes too far through the vein!

delicias hominis!
man love!
What a charm of...

Tarpeium limen adora pronus,
The threshold of the rock Tarpeya adores kneeling.

et auratam Iunoni caede iuuencam,
and, in honor of Juno, a heifer with golden horns a heifer
sacrifices.

si tibi contigerit capitis matron pudici.
if you had the luck of a chaste woman.

paucae adeo Cereris uittas contingere dignae,
There are very few worthy of reaching their hands to the
ribbons of Ceres,

quarum non timeat pater oscula.
and whose kisses his father does not fear.

prodigia et mores urbis damnante Canopo.
Canope herself condemned the surprising customs of
Rome.

immemor illa domus et coniugis atque sororis nil patriae
indulsit,
and forgetting about her house, her husband and her sister,
she didn't worry about anything for the country;

plorantisque improba natos utque magis stupeas ludos
Paridemque reliquit.
and her tearful children of her the evil one, and, what is even
more amazing, she gave up Paris and the circus games.

sed quamquam in magnis opibus paterna
And although in the midst of great opulence of the paternal
house

plumaque et segmentatis dormisset paruula cunis,
she as a child she had slept as a child among feathers and
in a golden cradle and although as a child

contemplate pelagus;
she despised the dangers of the sea

Famam contempserat olim,
as she had despised her reputation,

cuius apud molles minima est iactura cathedras.
whose sacrifice costs little to those accustomed to soft
armchairs.

si iubeat coniunx, durum est conscendere nauem,
If the husband orders it, it is hard to embark;

tunc sentina grauis, tunc summus uertitur aer:
then the bilge stink bothers, everything revolves around,

quae moechum sequitur, stomacho ualet.
but when she follows a lover, her stomach feels good.

illa maritum conuomit,
that one vomits on her husband;

haec inter nautas et prandet et errat per puppem
with this one (the lover), among the sailors they eat, walk
along the stern,

et duros gaudet tractare rudentis.
they entertain themselves by pulling the ropes.

qua tamen exarsit forma,
What guy has embraced Epia,

Qua capta iuuenta Eppia?
what youth has seduced her?

quid uidit propter quod ** ludia dici sustinuit?
What did she see so that gladiator keeps dedicating herself?

nam Sergiolus iam radere guttur coeperat
Well, Sergio has begun to shave his Adam's apple

et secto requiem sperare lacerto;
and to wait for her rest because of her arm that was cut off;

praeterea multa in facie deformia,
she showed her face full of flaws,

sicut attritus galea mediisque in naribus ingens gibbus
as if abused by her helmet in the middle of her nose, a big hump

et acre malum semper stillantis ocelli.
and a pungent humor that distilled from one eye.

sed gladiator erat.
But he was a gladiator!

facit hoc illos Hyacinthos;
That's enough to turn them into Hyacinths

hoc pueris patriaeque, hoc praetulit illa sorori atque uiro.

and give them preference over the country, over the children, over the sister and over the husband.

quid priuata domus, quid fecerit Eppia, cures?
Do you care about what an Epia does in a private house?

respice riuales diuorum,
For now see the rivals of the goddesses,

Suetonius narrates the alleged prostitution of the Empress Messalina.

Claudius audi quae tulerit.
listen to what Claudio has endured.

dormire uirum cum senserat uxor,
when the wife had realized that she was sleeping (relative + past imperfect) her husband,

sumere nocturnal meretrix Augusta (cucullos)
She wore two cloaks at night, the august whore.

(ausa) Palatino et tegetem (praeferre) cubili
daring to prefer a pallet to his bed on the Palatine

linquebat committee ancilla non amplius una.
and she left him in the company of a slave from her retinue.

sed nigrum flauo crinem abscondente galero
with black hair hidden under a blonde wig,
* sed, conjunction, but,(in a negative sentence), with

everything.
intrauit calidum ueteri centone (lupanar)
I entered the warm (brothel) of old mattresses

et cellam uacuam atque suam;
and in an empty room reserved for her.

tunc nuda papillis prostitit auratis
then with her bare golden breasts she prostituted herself

titulum mentita Lyciscae
under the false name of Licisca

ostenditque tuum, generose Britannice, uentrem.
and the wind showed that you, generous British (both in vocative).

(...)

nulla(ne) of tantis gregibus tibi digna uidetur?
Perhaps none, of such a worthy amount, do you think?

sit formonsa, decens, diues, fecunda,
be beautiful, well formed, rich, fruitful,

uetustos porticibus disponat auos,
that in the porches portraits of her ancestors place;

intactior omni crinibus effusis bellum dirimente Sabina,
purer than a Sabina with her hair down separating the combatants,

rara auis in terris nigroque (simillima) cycno,
very rare bird on Earth, (comparable) to a black swan;

quis feret uxorem cui constant omnia?
everything has it. Who would bear her as her wife?

quae tanti grauitas, quae forma, ut se tibi semper inputet?
What virtue or what beauty is worth so much to always
attribute it to?

huius enim rari summique uoluptas nulla boni
indeed, the satisfaction(voluptas) of this rare and supreme
good nothing(s)

quotiens animo corrupta superbo plus aloas quam mellis
habet.
how many times an altered and arrogant mood has more
bitterness than sweetness

quis deditus autem usque adeo est, ut non illam quam
laudibus
Who is actually devoted to such an extent to the one whom
he praises

effert horreat inque diem septenis oderit horis?.
that does not respond with fear for seven hours a day.?

quaedam parua quidem, sed non toleranda maritis.
some small things, no doubt, but that a husband does not
tolerate.
some trifles.

nam quid rancidius quam quod se non putat ulla formosam
Well, what is more unbearable in a woman who only
considers herself beautiful

nisi quae de Tusca Graecula facta est,
if, of Tuscan origin, it has become Greek,

of Sulmonensi mera? Omnia Grace:
though (is)* genuine from Sulmona? Everything (does) in
Greek,

cum sit turpe magis nostris nescire Latine.
as it would be more shameful in ours to ignore Latin.
being more embarrassing
When is...

hoc sermone pauent, hoc iram, gaudia, curas,
In this language (they express) their terror, their joys, their
eagerness;

hoc cuncta effundunt animi secreta.
through this (tongue) all the secrets of his heart are poured
out.

quid ultra? concumbunt Graece.
what else: even when they go to bed, (they do) in Greek.
What next

dones tamen ista puellis,
however give these fashions to young people.

tu(ne) etiam, quam sextus et octogensimus annus pulsat,

adhuc Graece?
perhaps you also in Greek, at your eighty years, when they
knock on your door?

non est hic sermo pudicus in uetula.
It's not this modest tongue on an old lady.

si tibi legitimis pactam iunctamque tabellis,
If through legitimate contact he has given you his faith and
joined you,

not es amaturus,
you must not love her (you must love her),

ducendi nulla uidetur causa,
to get married there is no reason,

nec est quare cenam
nor why splurge on a dinner

et mustacea perdas labente officio crudis donanda,
and in drunken biscuits that must be given to the guests,

nec illud quod prima pro nocte datur,
nor what is given for the first night,

si tibi simplicitas uxoria,
But yes, from your simplicity as a husband,

deditus uni est animus,
delivered to one is your wish,

summitte caput ceruice parata ferre iugum.
subdues the head and prepares the neck to bear the yoke.

nullam inuenies quae parcat amanti,
You will not find anyone who looks for the one who loves her,

ardeat ipsa licet,
that she herself burns she is allowed,

tormentis gaudet amantis et spoliis;
The one she loves she enjoys tormenting him and despoiling him;

igitur (longe) minus utilis illi uxor,
thus by far the least profitable to that woman,

(quisquis) erit bonus optandusque maritus.
the husband will be (the more) good and desirable.

nil umquam inuit donabis coniuge,
You can never give anything from her without her opinion,

uendes hac obstante nihil,
nor sell if she objects,

nihil haec si nolet emetur.haec dabit affectus:
nor buy if she does not want, she will give you her affections.

imperat ergo uiro.
therefore send the husband.

sed mox haec regna relinquit,
But soon this reign abandons,

permutatque domos et flammea conterit;
he will change houses, and the veil will trample (tear);

inde auolat et spreti repetit uestigia lecti.
from there she flies and from the bed that she despised she searches again for the traces.

(...)

i nunc et dubita qua sorbeat aera sanna maura,
Now go and doubt the grimace with which Tulia sips the air, what Maura says,

(...)

conuiuae miseri interea somnoque fameque urguentur.
Her guests, unhappy, meanwhile are dying of sleep and hunger.

tandem illa uenit rubicundula, totum oenophorum sitiens,
Finally, she arrives somewhat suffocated with the desire to drink the entire barrel,

plena quod tenditur urna admotum pedibus,
because, full, it was found at his feet with the contents of an urn;

de quo sextarius alter ducitur ante cibum rabidam facturus
orexim,
before eating, he will take another sextary drink that will
make his...
before eating, (ante... orexim).

dum redit et lotus terram ferit gut.
while he returns and washed the intestine, he hits the
ground staining the ground with vomit.
while it is going to stop, it returns(returns) and washed the
intestine

marmoribus riui properant, aurata Falernum peluis olet;
Rivers of wine run through the marble and the golden basin
stinks of Falerno;

nam sic, tamquam alta in dolia longus deciderit serpens,
bibit et uomit.
like a long snake fallen to the bottom of a barrel, it drinks
and vomits.

ergo maritus nauseat atque oculis bilem substringit opertis.
Her husband feels nauseated and closes his eyes to hold
back the bile.

illa tamen grauior, quae cum discusse coepit laudat
Vergilium,
that one, however more unbearable (is)* when she began to
lie down at the table.

laudat Vergilium
praise Virgil

periturae ignoscit Elissae,
to Dido willing to die, she forgives,
*

committit uates et comparat,
to the poets, and she compares them;

inde Maronem atque alia parte in trutina suspendit
Homerum.
from there to Virgilio Marón and on the other side of the
scale he hung Homer.

cedunt grammatici, uincuntur rhetores,
He puts the grammarians to retreat, he defeats the
rhetoricians,

omnis turba tacet, nec causidicus nec praeco loquetur,
altera nec mulier.
everyone is silent, not a lawyer, not a town crier, not another
woman,

uerborum tanta cadit uis,
so many words that falls;

tot pariter pelues ac tintinnabula dicas pulsari.
all at the same time boilers and hoods is pressed.

iam nemo tubas, nemo aera fatiget:
neither the trumpet nor the timpani persecutes anyone,
*Note.Possible sexual allusion.

una laboranti poterit succurrere Lunae.
she alone could help the Moon in danger,

inponit finem sapiens et rebus honestis;
she is the one who measures, even in honest things,

nam quae docta nimis cupit et facunda uideri
for she who too learned and eloquent wishes to appear,

crure tenus medio tunicas succingere debet.
must gird the tunic up to the middle of the leg,

caedere Siluano porcum, quadrante lauari.
immolate a pig to Silvano and take a bath for a quadrant

House of Casti Amanti,Pompeii.

Venus and Marte.House of Marte and Veneri, Pompeii.

MARTIAL. SOME EPIGRAMMS:

Chastity

53 [54]

Formosissima quae fuere uel sunt,
Catula, the most beautiful of all those who were or are,

sed uilissima quae fuere uel sunt,
but also the most despicable of all those who were or are,

o quam te fieri, Catulla, uellem formosam minus aut magis
pudicam!
how I would like you to become less beautiful or more
chaste,

67
Lascivam tota possedi nocte puellam,
I had with me for a whole night a lascivious young woman,

cuius nequitias vincere nulla potest.
whose pranks none is able to overcome.

fessus mille modis illud puerile poposci:
Tired of him in a thousand ways, I asked him about the
young people:
*Refers to anal sex.

ante preces totas prima que verba dedit.
before I finished my request and at my first words, he
granted it to me.

inprobius quiddam ridensque rubensque rogavi:
Between laughter and blushes, I asked for a more daring
thing:

pollicitast nulla luxuriosa mora.
she said that she was the lecherous one, without thinking
for a moment.

sed mihi pura fuit; tibi non erit, Aeschyle, si vis
But she with me was clean; I won't stay with you, Aeschylus,
if you want
* Reference to the fact that she did not have vaginal sex,
therefore, the young woman did not lose her "virginity of
hers".

accipere hoc munus conditione mala.
accept this gift on a bad condition.

Marriage of convenience

XXIII
Nubere Sila (feminine) mihi nulla non lege parata est;
Sila is willing to marry me under conditions;

sed Silam nulla ducere lege volo.
but I don't want to marry Sila on condition.

Cum tamen instaret, "deciens mihi dotis in auro
However, as she insisted, (I said: You will give me) a million
gold as a dowry as a wife.

(sponsa dabis" dixi. "Quid minus esse potest?"
  least could it be her?

"Nec futuam quamvis prima te nocte maritus,
  I will not do it (have sex) as a husband even the first night,

communis tecum nec mihi lectus erit;
and I will have no fellowship with you.

complectarque meam, nec you prohibit, amicam,
And I will hug my lover and you will not forbid me,

ancillam mittes et mihi iussa tuam.
and, when I command you, you will send me your slave.

te spectante dabit nobis lasciva minister basia,
Before your very eyes, she will give me lascivious kisses a
young slave,

sive meus sive erit ille tuus.
if he is mine as if he is yours.

Ad cenam venies, sed sic divisa recumbes,
You will come to dinners, but you will lie down at the table
so distant,

ut non tangantur pallia nostra tuis.
that my mantle does not touch with yours.

Oscula rara dabis nobis et non dabis ultro,
You will give me a kiss from time to time, and you will not give it to me on your own initiative,

nec quasi nupta dabis sed quasi mater anus.
neither will you give it to me as if you were my wife, but as if you were my old mother.

si potes ista pati, si nil perferre recusas,
If you can take this, if you can't resist taking it all,

Invenies qui te ducere, Sila, velit."
you will find, Sila, who wants to marry you

Prostitution

XIV
Ad nocturnal iaces fastosae limina moechae,
you spend your nights stretched out in front of the doorway of a luxury prostitute,

Et madet*, heu, lacrimis ianua surda tuis,
and her door, oh, deaf, is drenched in your tears,

Urere nec miserum cessant suspiria pectus.
and the sighs do not stop burning your poor heart.

Vis dicam, male sit cur tibi, Cotta? bene est
Do you want me to tell you why things are going badly for you, Cota?: You are doing well

63
Sola tibi fuerant sestertia, Miliche, centum,
You had but a hundred thousand sesterces, Milico,

quae tulit e sacra Leda redempta uia.
that Leda cost you, redeemed from the Sacred Way.
*Place where prostitutes were exhibited in search of clients.

Miliche, luxuria est si tanti diues amare.
Milico, even if you were rich, love at such a price would be a luxury.

'Non amo' iam you say: haec quoque luxuria est.
"I don't love her", you will say then. This too is a luxury.

12

Nulli, Thai, negates;
You deny yourself to no one, Tais;

sed si te non pudet istud,
but if that doesn't embarrass you,

hoc saltem pudeat, Thai, negare nihil.
at least be ashamed, Tais, of not denying yourself anything.

5.6
Comoedi tres sunt*, sed amat tua Paula, Luperce, quattuor:
There are three comedians, but your Paula loves four, Luperco

... * Paula ... love.
Paula also loves the mute character
*Written in Greek.

Taste for the forbidden

73

Nullus in urbe fuit tota qui tangere uellet
There wasn't one in the whole city who wanted to touch

uxorem gratis, Caeciliane, tuam, dum licuit:
to your wife, Ceciliano, while it was possible for free;

sed nunc positis custodibus ingens
but now that you have put guards on it,

turba fututorum est:
they are a troupe of lovers

ingenious homo is.
You are an ingenious man.

79

Rem peragit nullam Sertorius, inchoat omnes:
Sertorius does not finish a single matter and he begins all
of them.

hunc ego, cum futuit, non puto perficere.
This one, when he makes love, I don't think he'll go all the
way.

GREEK CULTURE REACHES THE MOST INTIMATE MOMENTS

JUVENAL.SATIRE

68
Cum tibi non Ephesos nec sit Rhodos aut Mitylene,
Although you do not have in Ephesus, nor in Rhodes, nor in Mytilene,

Sed domus in vico, Laelia, patricio,
your house, Lelia, but in the Patricio neighborhood

Deque coloratis numquam lita mater Etruscis,
and although your mother, who never wore makeup, is one of the red Etruscan

Durus Aricina from regione pater;
and your rustic father from the region of Aricia,

Kêri mou, mli mou, cuxæ mou congeris usque,
You have me fed up with so much "my owner, my honey, my heart."

Pro pudor!, Hersiliae civis et Egeriae.
What a shame! A compatriot from Hersilia and from Egeria!

Lectulus has voces, nec lectulus audiat omnis,
Let these words be heard by the bed, and not just any bed,

Sed quem lascivo stravit amica viro.
but the one that mistresses have prepared for lascivious men.

Scire cupis quo casta modo matrona loquaris?
Do you wish to know how to speak, chaste matron?

Numquid, cum crisas, blandior esse potes?
Is it that, when you move so awkwardly, you can be more seductive?

Tu licet ediscas totam referasque Corinthon,
You, as much as you refer to Corinth and try to imitate it entirely,

Non tamen omnino, Laelia, Lais eris.
however, Lelia, you will not be a Lais at all.

nam quid rancidius quam quod se non putat ulla formosam
Well, what is more unbearable in a woman who only considers herself beautiful

nisi quae de Tusca Graecula facta est,
if, of Tuscan origin, it has become Greek,

of Sulmonensi mera? omnia Grace:
though (is)* genuine from Sulmona? Everything (does) in Greek,

cum sit turpe magis nostris nescire Latine.
as it would be more shameful in ours to ignore Latin.
being more embarrassing

hoc sermone pauent, hoc iram, gaudia, curas,
In this language (they express) their terror, their joys, their desires;

hoc cuncta effundunt animi secreta.
through this (tongue) all the secrets of his heart are poured
out.

quid ultra? concumbunt Graece.
what else: even when they go to bed, (they do) in Greek.
What next

dones tamen ista puellis,
however give these fashions to young people.

tu(ne) etiam, quam sextus et octogensimus annus pulsat,
adhuc Graece?
perhaps you also in Greek, at your eighty years, when they
knock on your door?

non est hic sermo pudicus in uetula.
It's not this modest tongue on an old lady.

INCESTUOUS RELATIONSHIPS

Incest was used as a weapon of disrepute to bring down political rivals, denounced to the censors for carrying out this type of dishonest activity, they would be immediately crossed out with a note of infamy, losing their citizen rights. So Clodius accused Cicero's sister-in-law of having incestuous relationships.

Enemies with Cicero for this fact, when the speaker participated as a defense attorney for Celio, accused by Clodius's sister of trying to poison her, Cicero also insinuated that both brothers had incredible relationships.

Tacit. Annals.
About Emperor Nero's relationship with his own mother, Agrippina.

Tradit Cluvius ardore retinendae Agrippinam potentiae eo usque provectam, ut medio diei, cum id temporis Nero per vinum et epulas incalesceret,
-Cluvius writes that Agrippina, with the ardent desire she had to preserve her greatness, reached such a conclusion that when the day had passed, Nero was more excited with food and wine, and finally drunk,
-Cluvius relates that Agrippina, in her passion to conserve her power, reached such a point that in broad daylight, at a time when Nero was excited by the wine and the banquet,

offerret se saepius temulento comptam in incesto paratam; iamque lasciva oscula et praenuntias flagitii blanditias adnotantibus proximis,

-she visited him many times she offered herself groomed
and prepared to commit abominable incest with him, and
that seeing those who were close to her by her dishonest
kisses and lascivious caresses,
the messengers of such an ugly crime,
-she offered herself several times to her drunken son, very
neat and disposed to incest; that when those who were by
her side noticed her lascivious kisses and tenderness,
precursors of infamy,

Senecam contra muliebris inlecebras subsidium a femina
petivisse, immissamque Acten libertam, quae simul suo
periculo et infamia Neronis
-Seneca, against her womanly gifts, had sought remedies
that were also womanly, causing the freedwoman Acte,
showing herself distressed, not less at Nero's infamy than
at her own danger,
-Seneca sought help against the arts of that female in
another woman, bringing in the freedwoman Acte; that the
latter, disturbed both by the danger she ran and by the
prince's infamy,

anxia deferret pervulgatum esse incestum gloriante matre,
nec toleraturos milites profani principis imperium.
-I told her: that her incest was already widely publicized; that
her mother was proud of it, and that the soldiers were not
willing to put up with a prince who despised religion.
-she would warn him that the rumor of incest, of which her
mother gloried, had spread, and that the army would not
tolerate the rule of a sacrilegious prince.

Fabius Rusticus non Agrippinae sed Neroni cupitum id

memorat eiusdemque libertae astu disiectum.
-Fabius Rusticus says that this desire was not born of
Agrippina, but of Nero, and that it was separated from him
by cunning of the same freedwoman.
-Fabius Rusticus narrates that this was not Agrippina's wish,
but Nero's, and that everything was frustrated by the skill of
the freedwoman herself.

sed quae Cluvius, eadem ceteri quoque auctores prodidere,
et fame huc inclinat,
-But in what Cluvius writes the other authors agree, to which
fame also leans;
-Now then, the version of Cluvius is also that of the other
authors, and fame also leans in this direction,
*fame, rumour, public, common or majority opinion

seu concepit animo tantum immanitatis Agrippina, seu
credibilior novae libidinis meditatio in ea visa est, quae
puellaribus annis stuprum cum [M.] Lepido spe
dominationis admiserat,
-or because Agrippina had conceived in her mind a desire
so disordered and so contrary to nature, or because any
sensual appetite is more credible in a woman who in her
childhood years, moved by the desire to command, had
consented to the dishonest appetites of I ask,
-either because Agrippina really conceived in her mind so
much of her monstrosity, and because the invention of such
a novel passion seemed more credible in the one who in her
youthful years had committed rape with Lepidus for
ambition of power,

pari cupidine usque ad libita Pallantis provoluta et exercita
ad omne flagitium patrui nuptiis.

-giving herself later for the same cause to Palante, and accustomed to any evil since she married her uncle.

-in whom she with similar concupiscence she had lowered herself to satisfy the desires of Palante, and in whom she had exercised herself for all kinds of infamies by her marriage with her own uncle

Catullus

Incest.Ad Gellium LXXIV.

Gellius audierat patruum obiurgare solere,
Gellius had heard that her uncle used to censure him,

si quis delicias diceret aut faceret.
to whom he spoke or devoted himself to the enjoyment of it,

hoc ne ipsi accidentet, patrui perdepsuit ipsam
So that this would not happen to himself, she rubbed her own

uxorem, et patruum reddidit Arpocratem.
her uncle's wife and turned him into a Harpocrates.

quod voluit fecit: nam, quamvis irrumet ipsum
What he wanted he got: well, although now he gives it to his own to suck

nunc patruum, verbum non faciet patruus.
Uncle, this one won't say a word.

Incest.Ad Gellium

LXXXVIII.

Quid facit is, Gelli, qui cum matre atque sorore [prurit]*
What does Gelio do, the one who gets rid of itching with his mother and sister

[*], et abiectis pervigilat tunicis?
and he spends the night awake with his tunic removed?

quid facit is, patruum qui non sinit esse maritum?
What does he do who doesn't let his uncle be a husband? [who sodomizes his uncle]

ecquid scis quantum suscipiat sceleris?
Do you know what great crime he commits?

suscipit, o Gelli, quantum non ultima Tethys
Make one so big, Gellius, that not even distant Tethys

nec genitor Nympharum abluit Oceanus:
nor Oceanus, the father of the Nymphs, can wash it:

nam nihil est quicquam sceleris, quo prodeat ultra,
because there is no crime that goes further,

non si demisso se ipse voret capite.
not even if lowered the head it devours itself.

More on incest.Ad Gellium

LXXXIX.

Gellius est tenuis: quid ni? cui tam bona mater

Gelio is consumed: why not? of whom such a good mother

tamque valens vivat tamque venusta soror
and she so robust she lives her, and a sister so attractive,

tamque bonus patruus, tamque omnia plena puellis
[cognatis]*
and such a hot guy, and all around him is so full of young
cousins,

[*], what is the purpose of this macer?
how is this going to stop being emaciated?

qui ut (nihil) attingat, (nisi quod) fas tangere non est,
Although nothing reaches but what is not allowed to touch,

quantumvis quare sit macer invenies.
all the reasons you want why he is skinny you will find.

Incest with his mother. Ad Gellium

XC.

Nascatur magus ex Gelli matrisque nefando
Let a magician be born from the nefarious union of Gellius
and his mother

coniugio et discat Persicum aruspicium:
and learn the Persian art of divination:

nam magus ex matre et gnato gignatur oportet,
for it is necessary that a magician be begotten by a mother
and her son,

si vera est Persarum impia religio,
If the sacrilegious religion of the Persians is true,

gratus ut accepto veneretur carmine divos
so that he venerates the gods with pleasing prayers

omentum in flamma pingue liquefaciens.
(while) melting a greasy caul in the flames.

Ad Aufilenam CXI
Aufilena, viro contentam vivere solo,
Aufilena, to live content with only one man,

nuptarum laus ex laudibus eximiis:
of the married ones it is glory of privileged distinction;

sed cuivis quamvis potius succumbere par est,
but sleeping with anyone and as much as you want is better
than you,

quam matrem fratres efficere ex patro...
As a mother, beget cousins from your uncle.

Martial. Epigrams
4
O quam blandus es, Ammiane, matri!
Oh, Amiano, how affectionate you are with your mother!

quam blanda is tibi mater, Ammiane!

How loving your mother is to you, Ammianus!

Fratrem te uocat et soror uocatur.
She calls you brother, and you call her sister.

Cur uos nomina nequiora tangunt?
Why do you fancy those suspicious names?

Quare non iuuat hoc quod estis esse?
Why don't you like to be what you are?

Lusum creditis hoc iocumque? Non est:
Do you think this is a game and a joke? It is not:

matrem, quae cupit esse se sororem,
a mother who wants to be a sister,

nec matrem iuuat esse nec sororem.
she is not content to be a mother or a sister.

16
Priuignum non esse tuae te, Galle, nouercae rumor erat,
Rumor had it that you, Galo, were not a stepson to your stepmother

Coniunx dum fuit illa patris.
while she was your father's wife.

Non tamen hoc poterat uiuo genitore probari:
But this could not be proven living your parent.

iam nusquam pater est, Galle, nouerca domi est.

Your father has already disappeared, Galo, and the stepmother is still at your house.

Magnus ab infernis reuocetur Tullius umbris et te defendat Regulus ipse licet,
Even if the great Cicero of the infernal shadows is called back and Regulus himself defends you,

non potes absolui:
you cannot be acquitted!

nam quae non desinit esse post patrem, numquam, Galle, nouerca fuit.
A stepmother who does not stop being a stepmother when her father, Galo, dies, was never a stepmother.
*noverca novercae, stepmother.

Portrait of a Bacchante.

House of the cryptoportico.Pompeii.
In Greek mythology, the maenads are the nymphs who take care of the god Dionysus while he was a child, and with whom he had carnal relations, which caused them a kind of madness or mystical ecstasy.

They are assimilated with the bacchantes or worshipers of the god Bacchus who ingest hallucinogenic substances, raw meat, self-violence, and group sex among women.

BACCHANALIA

The **Bacchanalia** were festivals in honor of the god **Bacchus** (**Dionysus**, Greek).
Their priestesses were called bacchantes. They were secret rituals in which only women participated, they were performed in a grove near Mount Aventino on March 16 and 17 of each year. Later, it was extended to men and the celebrations took place five times a month.
The union of Bacchus with the god Pan and his fertility rites gave the cult a feminine orientation, the bacchantes were the worshipers of the god Bacchus.
In Italy, the cult originates in the colonies of Magna Graecia (southern Italy) and becomes very durable.
The mystery rituals to Dionysus/Bacchus have their origin in the myth of Orpheus. The beautiful musician was walking through the mountains of Thrace and a group of women dedicated to the cult of Dionysus harass him. Orpheus rejects his love claims because he took a vow of chastity after failing to rescue Eurydice from Hades.
The maenads (bachantes) very upset, come to rape him and kill him.
A bacchanal was thus the representation of the death of Orpheus at the hands of the priestesses of Dionysus.

Both matrons (women with older children) and maidens (single girls) walked through the woods for days, playing flutes and tambourines, and without contact with any man, they danced naked and performed rituals aided by alcohol and hallucinogenic herbs to reach such an ecstasy that they would reach a kind of mystical copulation with the deity that would serve them to obtain future fertility.

According to Euripides in his tragedy The Bacchae, the ritual was divided into three parts:

• women's retreat to the forest
• paroxysm or mystical ecstasy caused by drugs and group suggestion
• sacrifice of the animal that represents Dionysus (Pan) and the death of Orpheus, finally, they eats the raw meat from it.

Secrecy was inherent to all mystery cults, such as the bacchanals, so it is possible that in that altered state they performed different lesbian acts.

In Rome, a freed courtesan in love with the young knight, Ebucius, she reveals to him the secret of these rituals. Before his manumission, he accompanied his mistress and witnessed all kinds of crimes there.

The young man's father, a Roman knight, had died in the wars against Carthage and, since then, her mother and her new husband have dedicated themselves to squandering the estate. Both want to initiate Ebucius in the cult of Bacchus, since they offered him as a vow to the god for the recovery of the boy's weak health, but his real intention was something else, to make him lose his paternal inheritance. Warned of all this, Ebucius refuses to participate and tells what happened to the consul Postumius.

According to Titus Livy in book 39 of Ab Urbe Condita, the freedwoman tells the Consul that, in its beginnings, the cult of Bacchus was reserved only for women, who met two days a year, but a priestess from Campania began to initiate men and the nocturnal ceremonies passed to five per month.

Livy adds that:

"there was no crime or immorality that had not been committed there... only those under twenty were initiated, as they were more permeable to deceit and corruption... among them were some nobles... There was a great panic throughout the city,...and terror spread throughout Italy...many were caught trying to escape...Others, men and women, committed suicide...It was said that more than seven a thousand people".

The Senate feared that the practices of the sect could result in a real conspiracy against the Republic.

The year 186 BC. the Senatus consultum de Bacchanalibus was dictated by which bacchanals were prohibited throughout Italy (the meeting of more than five bacchantes), except in special circumstances that had to be approved by the Senate.

Apparently, the fear caused by three successive defeats before Carthage, leads to the reflection that introducing the cult of foreign divinities can motivate the discontent of the ancient gods, gods who would have turned their backs on Rome before their enemies; and they put the Republic in an extremely serious situation.

During the long wars against Carthage, women learned to live more independently, manage their property, claim their rights: in 195 B.C. they manage to repeal the Opia law, which limited their clothing and beads in public, as well as the use of carriages, in the face of the old tradition of Cato.

VENERALIA

In the month of April the feast of **Fortuna Virilis** was celebrated (**Veneralia**) in honor of Fortune and **Venus**

Verticordia (the one who opens our hearts to love).
This festival was established after consulting the oracle of
the Sibyl about the failures in the first war against Carthage,
attributed to the displeasure of the gods for the crimes
committed by some vestals, found lying with some males.
The goddess Fortuna was carried by women to public baths.
There the assistants undressed, and the prostitutes were
allowed to join married women to clean the statue of the
goddess and offer her roses. They all drank a drink made
from milk, honey, mint and hallucinogenic herbs, which was
consumed at the wedding of Venus and Vulcan.

They made offerings in the temple of Venus Ericina on the
day of **Vinalia,** festival in honor of wine.
On April 25 the **pueri lenonii** (homosexual prostitutes)
celebrated the **Robigalia** festival.
On April 27, the festival was celebrated in honor of the
goddess Flora (**Floralia**) where the prostitutes danced
sensually moving their hips and showed her naked body.

SEX GODS

Priapus

God worshiped by shepherds and peasants. He was the
guardian of the gardens and orchards. He protected against
the evil eye and envy.
He was represented as a tree trunk in which a reddish stake
was stuck, symbolizing a huge erect phallus. He was placed
in the graves as a protector of resurrection and immortality.

A **tintinnabulum** was a bronze phallic-shaped bell or fascinum, a magical phallus that warded off curses and brought good luck and fortune.
from the evil eye and bring good fortune and prosperity. It was hung outdoors and the wind made it sound.

This same function was fulfilled by the ceramics or bronzes of one or several penises or the statuettes of the god of sexual vigor (**Priapus**) that were placed at the entrance door of houses or shops.

Mutuno Tutuno

God of manhood. He was represented with a phallus on which the bride had to sit on the wedding night, before the act to lose his virginity.
He was associated with Priapus. Protector of jealousy and envy.

Cinxia

Bridal goddess that on the wedding night, she loosened the girdle of the bride's dress, untying the magic knot that she had kept her virginity.
(Hercules knot or cingulum herculeum).

Cloacin

Sabine goddess of sexual pleasure and brutal passions.

Liburnum

God of sexual pleasure.

Bona Dea

Faun's wife. Goddess of fertility, model of virtue and chastity. One day she got drunk and was killed by her husband.
In honor of the Goddess a special cult was established.

Faun/Pan

Greek god (Arcadia region) of shepherds and flocks, of fertility and male sexuality, has similarities with Dionysus (Bacchus), he is identified with the Roman Faun.
He was a hunter and a musician, he scared the herds and everyone who came near.
He lived in the company of the nymphs in a cave of Parnassus, He chased the young women through the fields until they satisfied his carnal desires, he was part of Dionysus' courtship.

In the work the Satyricon of Petronius, a satirical writing from the times of Nero that has partially come down to us, different sexual activities of its protagonists are narrated: anal sex, orgies, sex toys, incestuous relationships.
The story tells of the adventures in the initial stage of the Roman Empire (most likely, before the end of the 1st century AD) of two young men, Encolpius and Ascyltus, as well as of the young lover of the first, the adolescent Giton.
Encolpius **has been punished by the god Priapus by making him victim of a sexual impotence.**

•Ascyltos has anal sex with Giton but Encolpius wants to be Giton's lover.
When Giton and Encolpius are in bed, Ascyltos interrupts them.
•Quartillas' maids and a prostitute sodomize the protagonists in an orgy.
•Giton has sex with a young woman.
•Eumolpus has anal sex with a boy from Pergamon until exhaustion.
•Circe sends her lesbian lover, Chrysis, to hint to Encolpius that Circe wants to have sex with him, but Encolpius can't get an erection.
frustrated at not feeling wanted, she has him flogged..
Encolpius despairs and thinks of cutting off his penis, but he **prays to Priapus in his temple to cure him,** then the priestess Enotea appears who affirms that she will remedy his illness and brings him a "leather dildo" (**olisbos or scorteum fascinum**) to which women apply an Encolpius lubricant for anal penetration.
Finally, she is cured of sexual impotence by having incestuous relationships, the cause of the greatest pride and infamy in his person.

SEXUAL LEXICON

Latin has a specific verb for each sexual act.
The infinitives to indicate the sexual act, appear in an active form (function of the male), and in a passive form (function of the woman).

-Futuo futui futum futuere (insert the penis into the vagina).
  It comes from the Greek fyteúoo (to engender, procreate) from the verb fýoo., (to cause to be born).
-Irrumo irrumaui irrumatum irrumare (put the penis in the mouth, humiliate someone).
- Paedico pedicare (insert the penis into the anus).
  It comes from the Greek paidikós, from paîs, paidós (child, young).

-Futui (to be penetrated in the vagina).
-Fellari/irrumari (to be penetrated or penetrated in the mouth).
  Fello fellaui fellatum (lick). The action can be active or passive.
-Pedicari (being penetrated or penetrated in the anus).

The Vir, male can be:
Fututor (vaginal penetrator).
Irrumator (oral penetrator).
Pedicator/pedico (anal penetrator).

The Femina or puella can be:
Fututa (vaginally penetrated).
Fellatrix/irrumata (orally penetrated).
Pathica/pedicata (anally penetrated).

Attingo, attigi (touch, feel).
LXXIV
Moechus erat: poteras tamen hoc tu, Paula, negare.
He was your lover, but you could deny that, Paula.

Ecce uir est: numquid, Paula, negare potes?
Now that he is your husband: can you deny it, Paula?

XVI

Pedicabo ego uos et irrumabo,
I will give you by the anus and by the mouth,
I will have sex with you by...

Aureli pathice et cinaede Furi,
Pederast and castaway Aurelio, Furio,

Qui me ex uersiculis meis putastis,
That you judged me for my little verses,

Quod sunt molliculi, parum pudicum.
Well, they are tender, little modest.
Martial. Epigrams.

Mars and Venus of the house of Meleager in Pompeii

Couple in bed.House of the Farnesina in Rome

POMPEII

Many of the frescoes, mosaics and sculptures that appeared in the cities of Pompeii and Herculaneum, buried by the ashes of Vesuvius, scandalized their first discoverers (the first excavations began between 1748 and 1750), so they were taken to the Naples museum.

In 1819 King Francis I, embarrassed by the explicit Roman art of Pompeii, ordered that these works be kept in a room of the museum, closed to the public, to which only scholars could access, and it remained so until the end of the century. XX.

Large-scale excavations of Pompeii began in 1860, and much of the erotic art came to light, shocking the intellectual heirs of the Roman Empire.

As they did not know what to do with these explicit sexual representations, the sculptures were moved to a closed room in the Archaeological Museum of Naples, and the objects that remained in Pompeii were covered again.

In Pompeii there are 35 dwellings whose walls contain erotic paintings.

In Latin brothel is lupanar, den of wolves, and the prostitute was called lupa ("she-wolf").

Lupanar or brothel

The Lupanar of Pompeii had 10 rooms. A mattress was placed on a brick structure.

The rooms were very small and had no doors or curtains. The sexual practices were carried out in full view of the other clients and prostitutes.

The price of the sexual act appears next to each door.

The erotic paintings were discovered in 1862, and are found in the corridors, near the ceiling.
There are seven well-preserved paintings:
5 represent the sexual act between a man and a woman.
Another fresco depicts the god of sexual vigour, Priapus, with his huge erect penis.
There are also merely decorative images.
There are no scenes of oral sex (**cunnilingus**) or anal sex.
In the paintings that are at the entrance, the breasts are hidden with the fascia pectoralis or bra.
The breasts are on view in the paintings that are located at the end of the corridor.

150 graffiti with texts (Latin and Greek) and drawings were discovered on the walls with all kinds of content: obscene, social and political life, greetings, poems.
Most are in the rooms closest to the front door:
Hic ego puellas fines futui ("Here I do it with many girls").
Felix bene futuis ("Lucky guy, you fuck well", apparently a prostitute's compliment to her client).
Likewise, in **Livia fellat** ("Livia sucks it"), which has an active meaning, instead of Livia irrumat (Livia sucks it off me), which has a passive meaning, it is regrettable that some graphics were written by women.
Sabino Proclo salutem ("Salute from Sabino to Proclus").
There are graphs written by children:
Africanus moritur scribe puer Rusticus condisce(n)s cui dolet pro Africano ("Africanus died. The boy Rusticus writes this. Who mourns the death of Africanus?").
The nobles did not usually go to this place, they had many slaves or paid mistresses (concubines).
Paintings with different sexual scenes were found on a wall in the suburban baths of Pompeii: anal sex, oral sex,

threesomes...

Suburban Hot Springs

To the southwest of Pompeii, outside the city, leaning on the wall and near the Marina gate and the road that led to the port, there are some so-called suburban baths.They measure about 800 square meters.

Although the baths have been known since 1959, their paintings only came to light in the late 1980s.
On the second floor there is a unique changing room (apodyterium) for men and women*, on one of whose walls 8 sexual scenes are represented: in a couple, a threesome and a foursome.
Beneath each scene there is a stone bench and lockers to put clothes, painted and numbered from 1 to 8.
These paintings from the time of Nero were covered before the eruption of 79 AD.
*In the Forum baths and in the Estabia baths there were two changing rooms.

The erotic paintings in the Suburban Baths of Pompeii are the only example of erotic art to be found in a public Roman bath.
They are located near the entrance, in the changing room (**apodyterium**) where there is a continuous bench and recessed niches in the wall and numbered in Latin, as lockers, to leave clothes and personal belongings, which were guarded by a slave.
Representing the sexual act was an inferior or degrading form of art, so it is not known whether its meaning was sexual arousal or a way to cause laughter or amuse visitors

to the place.

It must be taken into account that this locker room, as well as the rest of the facilities, was shared by men and women, so, according to experts, these scenes would have more of a humorous meaning than obscene or strictly sexual.

The images are as follows:

-**Heterosexual sex:** scenes I and II:
Two sexual acts between man and woman.
•Position of Venus pendula (Hector's Horse or cowgirl position).
• from the back (a tergo) lying on one side (semi-supine position).
-**Oral sex:**
•Scene III (fellatio).
  Woman giving to fellatio to a man.
•Scene IV(cunnilingus).
  Man performing cunnilingus on a woman.
-**Lesbian sex:**
•Scene V (couple in bed).
Two lesbians with a dildo in the form of a phallus
(**scorteum fascinum** or astonishment of prostitutes).
The hair indicates that this is a lesbian sex scene.
The woman on the right wearing a fascia pectoralis lies back on a bed.
-**Group sex:**
•Scenes VI (a sexual threesome)
  Two men and one woman (double anal sex).
•Scene VII, (a sexual foursome).
two men and two women.
-**Scene VII.**
Naked man with huge testicles.

Scene I   Scene VI

Scene I.the woman has her pubic hair completely shaved.

Scene VI.The woman on the left has her red pectoral fascia lowered and shows her right breast. The man supports her left hand on the woman's head.

Here we can see a women placed on top of the man
(Hector's house or cowgirl position).

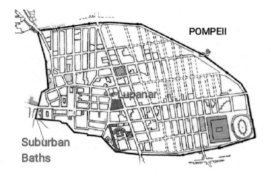

Map of Pompeii indicating the location of the suburban baths and the lupanar (brothel)

Suburban Baths   Lupanar

BIBLIOGRAPHY

-LUCIAN, Dialogues, True Stories, Planeta DeAgostini, Spain, 1998.

-OVID, Art of Loving. Amores, Planeta DeAgostini, Spain, 1997. -SUETONIUS, Life of the Twelve Caesars, Planeta DeAgostini, Spain, 1997.

-TACITUS, Annals, Ocean publishing group, Spain, 2000.

-ALFARO GINER, C. Weaving in Roman times, Arco Libros, Madrid, 1997.

-ALFÖLDY, Géza, Social History of Rome, Editorial Alliance, Madrid, Spain, 1987.

-ALMUDENA MARTÍN PÉREZ, Prostitution in Ancient Rome. Art and eroticism in ancient Rome in: Magazine of Archeology, No. 83, March 1988, Spain.

-BEJIN, A.; FOUCAULT, M.; Western sexualities, Editorial Paidós, 1987.

-CLARKE JOHN. Looking at lovemaking: constructions of sexuality in Roman, Berkeley: University of California Press.1998.

-CUATRECASAS, A., Eros in Rome, Madrid, 1993.

-ETIENNE, Robert, Daily life in Pompeii, Aguilar S.A. Madrid, Spain, 1971.

-FAYER, C. The Roman Family: Aspetti Giuridici ed Antiquari. Concubinage Divorce Adultery. L'Erma di Bretschneider, Rome, 2005.

-FERNÁNDEZ URIEL, P.; Workers and businesswomen in the High Imperial Roman Period, Space, Time and Form. Series II, Ancient History, 2011.

-FOUCAULT MICHEL, History of Sexuality.

-GARDNER, J.F., Women in Roman Law and Society, London, 1995.

-DILLON MATHEW; GARLAND LYNDA . Ancient Rome: From the Early Republic to the Assassination of Julius Caesar. Taylor & Francis.2005.

-GRANT MICHAEL; MULES ANTONIA.Eros in Pompeii: The Erotic Art Collection of the Museum of Naples. New York: Stewart, Tabori and Chang.1997.

-GREGORIO NAVARRO, Mª C. D.; Gender violence and deprivation of liberty in the classical world, in A. Domínguez Arranz and R. Mª Marina Sáez, Gender and the teaching of History, Sílex, Madrid, 2015.

-FAIRIES, MOSES, Imperial Rome, Echoes of Glory, Folio, Barcelona,1996.

-KIEFER, O., Sexual life in Ancient Rome, London, 1934.

-LICHT HANS, Sexual Life of Ancient Greece, FELMAR Editions, Abraxas Collection, Spain, 1976.

-MC GINN, THOMAS A.J., Prostitution, Sexuality and the Law in the Ancient Rome, New York, 1998.

-MC GINN THOMAS A.J. The Economy of Prostitution in the Roman World. Ann Arbor: The University of Michigan Press.2004.

-OLDENDORFF, ANTOINE, Corporality, sexuality and culture, Carlos Lohlé Editions. Argentina, 1970.

-ROBERT, J.N., Pleasures in Rome, Madrid, 1992.

-STEWART JUAN, The intimate life of the Romans and the Greeks, Spanish-American Ed., Madrid, Spain, 1985.

-URBANIK, J. Husband and Wife, in P. Du Plessis, C. Ando and K. 2016,
Tuori (editions).

-VARONE ANTONIO.Eroticism in Pompeii. Getty Trust Publications.2001.
 (J. Paul Getty Museum).

-VANOYEKE, V., Prostitution in Greece and Rome, Madrid, 1991.

-VEYNE, Paul, Homosexuality in Rome, in ARIES.
-VEYNE, Paul. The Roman Empire, Various Authors, History of Private Life.
-WILKINS, A.S. The daily life of the Romans (Roman Antiquities), Editorial ATALAYA, Argentina.

Pompeii and Greek Art.

-BERRY, J., Pompeya , Akal, Madrid, 2009.
-BADIA VILA, MªAMPARO; GARCÍA MIRANDA, ENRIQUETA(2014). Depilación mecánica y decoloración del vello . Madrid:Ediciones Paraninfo.2014.
-BEARD MARY. A nice bath.Pompeii: History and Legend of a Roman City. Crítica Barcelona, 2009.
-JACOBELLI, L., Le pitture erotiche delle terme Suburbane di Pompei. L'Erma di Bretschneider,
Roma, 1995.
-MAZZOLENI, D., PPALARDO, U., y ROMANO, L. Domus: Wall Painting in the Roman
House , Getty Trust Publications, J. Paul Getty Museum, 2005.
-CALAME, CLAUDE. Eros en la Antigua Grecia. Editorial Akal, España, 1992.
-DOVER, K.J. Homosexualidad griega . El Cobre Ediciones, España, 2008.
-Pompeian Amatorial Graffiti, Priapean, The Evening of the Feast of Venus, Planeta DeAgostini, Spain, 1997.
-Corpus Inscriptionum Latinarum.

Thanks

ica3.jpg
Deutsch: Cunnilingusszene; Pompejanische Wandmalerei, Vorstadt-Thermen, Südwand des Auskleideraums, um 79 v. Chr.Date 8 November 2006 (upload date).Source Own work.Author: **Fer.filol.**

-https://commons.m.wikimedia.org/wiki/File:Wall_painting_ -_love-making_in_the_bedroom_-_Pompeii_-_Napoli_MAN_2 7696.jpg
Wall painting (fresco) love-making in the bedroom with exuberant drapery.
Fourth style of pompeian (height: 54 cm width: 51 cm): findspot Pompeii.Napoli,Museo Archeologico Nazionale 27696.
Date 6 October 2018.Source Own work.Author: **ArchaiOptix.**

-https://commons.m.wikimedia.org/wiki/File:Wall_painting_ -_love_making_-_Pompeii_-_Napoli_MAN_27697.jpg
Wall painting (fresco) love making .
Third style of pompeian (height: 37 cm - width: 37)findspot Pompeii. Napoli, Museo Archeologico Nazionale 27697.Date 6 October 2018.Source Own work.Author: **ArchaiOptix**.

-https://commons.m.wikimedia.org/wiki/File:Wall_painting_ -_love_making_-_Pompeii_-_Napoli_MAN_27686.jpg
Wall painting (fresco) love making.
Third style of pompeian wall painting (height: 44 cm - width: 41cm) findspot: Pompeii. Napoli, Museo Archeologico Nazionale 27686
Date 6 October 2018.Source Own work.Author: **ArchaiOptix.**

-https://commons.m.wikimedia.org/wiki/File:Wall_painting_

-_love-making_-_Vesuvius_region_-_Napoli_MAN.jpg
Love-making on a kline.
Third style of pompeian wall painting, mid first century AD
(height: 39 cm - width: 49 cm) findspot: Vesuvius region,
probably from a lupanar.
Napoli, Museo Archeologico Nazionale
Date 6 October 2018.Source Own work.Author: **ArchaiOptix.!**

-https://commons.m.wikimedia.org/wiki/File:Pompeya_Erot
ica2.jpg
Erotic fresco found in the House of the King of Prussia
(VII.9.33) in the ancient city of Pompeii, currently exhibited
at the National Archaeological Museum of Naples, in the
rooms called the Secret Cabinet.
The painted Latin inscription, partially vanished, reads:
 "LE (NT) E IMPELLE", "Push slowly" it is a request from the
prostitute to the client on duty.
Date 7 November 2006 (upload date)Source Own
work.Author: **Fer.filol**

-https://commons.m.wikimedia.org/wiki/File:Pompei-grafiti
-S.jpg

日本語: ポンペイ娼館に残っていた壁画(縮小版)Date April

2001 Source Own work. Author: **Okc.**

-http://commons.wikimedia.org/wiki/File:Termas_Suburban
as_-_Apodyterium.JPG
-https://es.m.wikipedia.org/wiki/Archivo:Pittore_dell'angelo
volante(attr.),_anfora_con_falli-uccello_e_ragazza_con_un
_fallo,_490_ac._ca._04.JPG
Arte greca, Petit Palais, Parigi
Date, november 2013.Source, own work. Author,**Sailko**.

-https://commons.m.wikimedia.org/wiki/File:Pomperos23.
 jpg.English: Erotic scene (Pompeii)
Date 16 November 2002 (original upload date)
Source Transferred from en.wikipedia to Commons.
Author The original uploader was Eloquence at English
Wikipedia.

-https://es.m.wikipedia.org/wiki/Archivo:Villa_Romana_del_
Casale_Schlafzimmer_Mitte_modified.jpg
Eros e Psiche.Piazza Americana, Sizilien, Villa Romana del
Casale, ein Mosaik in dem Schlafzimmer (Privaträume) der
Hausherrin, es zeigt ein Liebespaar. Date, May 2006.Author:
Clemensfranz.

-https://es.m.wikipedia.org/wiki/Archivo:Casale_Bikini.jpg
Bikini mosaic, famous"bikini girls" mosaic (found by
archeological excavation of the ancient Roman villa near
Piazza Armerina in Sicily), showing women exercising,
running, or receiving the palm of victory and crown (for
winning an athletic competition).
Villa Romana del Casale.
Date June 2006.Source. M. Disdero.Author: **M. Disdero.**

-https://es.m.wikipedia.org/wiki/Archivo:Bikinimaedchen.jpg
bikinimädchen, römisches Mosaik in der Villa del Casale
(Sizilien) Date.2006. Author: **Pavel Krok.**

-https://commons.m.wikimedia.org/wiki/File:Casa_di_Caeci
lius_Jucundus_-_Peristyl_l_-_North_wall.jpg
Fresco of couple in bed. Fresko from the north wall of the
peristy   between rooms in the house of Caecilius Iucundus
(V 1, 26) in Pompeii. Museo Archologico nazionale, Neapel,

Inv. 110569.July 2010
Source John R. Clarke: Ars Erotica. Darmstadt: Primus 2009.
Author: **Wolfgang Rieger.**

-https://commons.m.wikimedia.org/wiki/File:Eroticpair.jpg
Wall Painting, House of the Epigrams, Reign of Nero. From
Pompeii, now in the Archaeological Museum in Naples (inv.
nr. 27705).
This file is lacking source information.

-https://commons.m.wikimedia.org/wiki/File:Fragment_of_
wall_painting_depicting_Mars_and_Venus,_from_the_House
_of_Meleager_in_Pompeii,_Naples_National_Archaeological
Museum(17136444089).jpg
Fragment of wall painting depicting Mars and Venus, from
the House of Meleager in Pompeii, Naples National
Archaeological Museum
Date July 2014, Author: **Carole Raddato** from FRANKFURT,
Germany
-https://commons.m.wikimedia.org/wiki/File:Pompeii_-_Ca
sa_di_Marte_e_Venere_-_MAN.jpg
Roman fresco of Venus and Mars from the Casa di Marte e
Venere (VII 9, 47) in Pompeii. Museo Archeologico
Nazionale (Naples).Date March 2009.Source Marisa Ranieri
Panetta (ed.): Pompeji. Geschichte, Kunst und Leben in der
versunkenen Stadt. Belser, Stuttgart 2005,
ISBN 3-7630-2266-X , p. 203.Author: **WolfgangRieger.**

-https://commons.m.wikimedia.org/wiki/File:Casa_della_Fa
rnesina_-_Cubiculum_D_-_Right_wall_-_Right_Side.jpg
Fresco of couple in bed. Now the bride appears to be quite
willing. A nude servant on the right looks to the side. Fresko
from the right side of the right wall of cubiculum D in the

Casa della Farnesina in Rome. 19 BC. Museo Nazionale Romano, Palazzo Massimo alle Terme, Inv. 1188.Date July 2010.Source **John R. Clarke: Ars Erotica. Darmstadt**: Primus 2009.Author **Wolfgang Rieger.**

-https://ca.m.wikipedia.org/wiki/Fitxer:Pompeii_-_Casa_dei _Casti_Amanti_-_Banquet.jpg
Roman fresco with banquet scene from the Casa dei Casti Amanti (IX 12, 6-8) in Pompeii.
Deutsch: Bankettszene. Römisches Fresko aus dem Haus der keuschen Liebenden (IX 12, 6-8) in Pompeji.
Data març de 2009.Source. **Marisa Ranieri Panetta (ed.): Pompeji**. Geschichte, Kunst und Leben in der versunkenen Stadt. Belser, Stuttgart 2005, ISBN 3-7630-2266-X , p. 206.Autor **WolfgangRieger.**

-https://es.m.wikipedia.org/wiki/Archivo:Clarke_Ars_Erotica _04.jpg
Southern wall of room 43 (Cubiculum) in the Casa del Centenario (IX 8,3) in Pompeii, 1st
Century. Fresco of couple in bed.
Date.July 2010. Source.**John R. Clarke: Ars Erotica. Darmstadt**: Primus 2009.Autor **Wolfgang Rieger.**

-https://commons.m.wikimedia.org/wiki/File:Musa_con_lira.jpg
Italiano: Affresco di Villa San Marco di una Musa di spalle mentre suona una lira.Source Own work.Author:
Mentnafunangann

-https://en.m.wikipedia.org/wiki/File:Bains_et_les_édifices_ sportifs_de_Pompéi.jpg

Les bains et les édifices sportifs Thermes suburbaines
Thermes du forum Thermes centrales Thermes de Stabies
Non renseigné Forum Triangulaire Palestre Samnite
Grande Palestre Lupanar.
Date 30 August 2007.Source From Image:PlanPompeji3.jpg.
Author fr:User:**Pseudomoi.**

-https://commons.m.wikimedia.org/wiki/File:Bronze_'flying
_phallus'_amulet.JPG
Bronze 'flying phallus' amulet, 1stC BC. It would be hung
outside a house or shop doorway to ward off evil spirits.
National Archaeological Museum, Naples.
Date 26 July 2012.Source Own work.**Kim Traynor.**

-https://en.m.wikipedia.org/wiki/File:Pompeya_lupanar.jpg
Lupanar en la ciudad de Pompeya
Date 8 November 2006 (upload date).Source Own
work.**Author Fer.filol.**

-https://en.m.wikipedia.org/wiki/File:Porta_Marina_(723883
5816).jpg
Suburban Baths near the Porta Marina
Date.May 2011.Source Porta Marina.Uploaded by Marcus
Cyron.Author **Dave & Margie Hill / Kleerup.**
Date.Julio de 2012.Author.**Kim Traynor.**

-https://en.m.wikipedia.org/wiki/File:Sexual_scene_on_pom
peian_mural_1.jpg
Paar beim Geschlechtsakt; Pompejanische Wandmalerei,
Vorstadt-Thermen, Südwand des Auskleideraums, um 79 v.
Chr.
Couple faisant l'amour. Fresque de Pompei, thermes, mur
sud de la salle de déshabillage, vers 79 avjc.

Source.**Angelika Dierichs**: Erotik in der Rmischen Kunst. von Zabern, Mainz 1993 (Zaberns Bildbnde zur Archeologie) ISBN 3-8053-1540-6.
Date.March 2006.Author **Marcus Cyron.**
-https://es.m.wikipedia.org/wiki/Archivo:In_situ_wall_fresco _with_erotic_scene_in_the_Lupanar_,_Pompeii_(146735030 07).jpg
ción In situ wall fresco with erotic scene in the Lupanar , Pompeii
Date July 2014. Source In situ wall fresco with erotic scene in the Lupanar , Pompeii.Author **Carole Raddato** from FRANKFURT, Germany

-https://en.m.wikipedia.org/wiki/File:Pompeii_-_Terme_Sub urbane_-_Apodyterium_-_Scene_V.jpg
Scene V of the famous mural showing variants of sexual intercourse. Couple in bed. The hair of the figure on the left indicates that this is a lesbian sex scene. The woman on the right wearing a fascia pectoralis lies back on a bed or a cline. The patches of dark green color are remains of the repainting of the wall.
Date 12 July 2010.Source **John R. Clarke:** Ars Erotica. Darmstadt: Primus 2009.Author **Wolfgang Rieger.**

-https://en.m.wikipedia.org/wiki/File:Pompeii_-_Terme_Sub urbane_-_Apodyterium.jpg
Part of the famous mural showing variants of sexual intercourse. Roman fresco from the Terme Suburbane in Pompeii.
Date March 2009.Source **Filippo Coarelli** (ed.): Pompeji. Hirmer, München 2002, ISBN 3-7774-9530-1 , p. 188.Author **WolfgangRieger**.

-https://en.m.wikipedia.org/wiki/File:Pompeii_-_Lupanar_-_
Erotic_Scene_-_MAN.jpg
Erotic Scene from the eastern side of the southern wall of
the Lupanar. Roman fresco in Pompeii.
Date 15 March 2009.Source **Filippo Coarelli** (ed.): Pompeji.
Hirmer, München 2002, ISBN 3-7774-9530-1 , p. 195.Author
WolfgangRieger.

Author's review.

The author, a Law graduate and passionate about culture and the classical world, has published Roma Aeterna on Kindle: an extensive collection of works on the Latin language and culture, written in English and Spanish. Among them we can highlight: Roman cuisine, its cuisine and its recipes; Roman culture, life in Rome, a journey through the classical world; Julius Caesar, Civil War, Gallic War, etc.

Fresco of Villa San Marco

Printed in Great Britain
by Amazon

24101515R10086